I0457817

# Far from Home

## A Practical Guide to Coping, Adapting, and Thriving Abroad

CK Franco

Copyright © [2025] by [Ck Franco]

All rights reserved.

No portion of this book may be reproduced in any form without written permission from the publisher or author, except as permitted by U.S. copyright law.

# *Blurbs*

**Far From Home: Working Abroad — A Realistic, Inspiring Survival Guide for Every Expat Dreamer**

Stepping into a new country is more than a journey—**it's a transformation**.

Whether you're moving abroad for opportunity, survival, love, or reinvention, this powerful guide shines a clear light on the *real* emotional, psychological, and practical challenges expats face every single day.

From the thrill of the unknown to culture shock, homesickness, identity loss, and rebuilding your life from zero, **Far From Home: Working Abroad** offers **honest stories, practical strategies, and deeply relatable insights** for anyone starting over in a foreign land.

If you've ever wondered...

*Will I belong there?*

*How do I deal with cultural differences?*

*What if I fail?*

*How do I rebuild a routine, friendships, and confidence?*

*How do other OFWs and expats survive the emotional rollercoaster?*

...this book gives you the roadmap.

Perfect for:

• Overseas Filipino Workers (OFWs)

• First-time expats

• Migrant families

• Digital nomads

• Anyone preparing for a life-changing move abroad

With heartfelt stories and grounded guidance, this book will help you **adapt, thrive, and rediscover who you are—far away from everything familiar.**

**If you're searching for strength, clarity, or courage before (or during) working abroad... this is the book you need.**

To every brave soul who left home to build a better life—
your courage, sacrifice, and unseen battles inspire the world.
This book is for you.

"Home is not a place—it is every version of ourselves we meet along the journey."

# Prologue

The night before her flight, Erin stood by the window of her nearly empty apartment, watching the familiar street below fade into a memory she hadn't even lived yet. Boxes lined the wall—small now compared to the weight of the decision she carried.

Friends told her she was brave. Family called her strong. But courage felt like a word made for someone else—someone who wasn't fighting the quiet fear inside her chest.

She wasn't running from her life.
She was running toward something she hoped existed.
A chance.
A reset.
A version of herself she had never met.

She knew the reality: working abroad wasn't a dream painted in glossy photographs. It was a thousand little uncertainties—new rules, new routines, new identities. But it was also possibility. It was reinvention.

As she zipped her final suitcase, Erin whispered a promise—not to the life she was leaving, but to the one waiting on the other side:

*"Whatever happens... I will find a way to belong."*

She had no idea how true, how messy, and how transformative that promise would become.

# Contents

# Into the Unknown: The Bold Leap Abroad

E rin sat quietly at her kitchen table, the morning light casting soft shadows across a stack of unopened mail. Her mind wandered as she sipped her coffee, grappling with the growing restlessness that had crept into her life unnoticed. The familiar rhythm of her days—the commute, the office walls, the weekend errands—suddenly felt confining, like invisible walls closing in. Meanwhile, friends spoke of adventures abroad, sharing tales filled with excitement and uncertainty, stirring a mix of longing and doubt within her. Questions swirled: What if leaving everything knownshe knew behind was a mistake? Could she handle the loneliness or the unexpected challenges waiting on foreign streets? In these moments of hesitation and hope, a quiet battle plays out inside many who stand at the edge of a new life far from home.

## Motivations and Emotional Preparation: Why We Leave and Facing Inner Doubt

Gray light filters through the half-open curtains as Erin sips her morning coffee, already sensing a hollowness in the predictability of her day ahead. The same commute, the same faces, the same calendar reminders blinking at her. She cannot ignore the constant tap on her shoulder—the urge to break free from the numbing cycle of routine. Like Erin, many adults reach a point when comfort begins to feel like a cage, suffocating the possibility for change. Underneath the calm surface of job stability, familiar neighborhoods, and weekend routines grows a persistent call for something deeper. The search for growth and reinvention starts with acknowledging this silent unrest.

Stagnation often builds slowly. Months pass, then years, and the small joys that once colored daily life lose their shine. For some, like Dan, a software engineer in his late thirties, the decision comes sharply one morning at his office desk. He realizes he can predict every task and every face in his weekly meetings. The idea of doing the same work for another decade terrifies him more than the thought of facing an uncertain future abroad. In these moments, many realize that the discomfort of venturing into the unknown feels more honest and promising than the slowly eroding comfort of routine.

A craving for deeper meaning propels many to consider life in a new country. Living abroad offers a chance to rewrite personal purpose, to test boundaries, and, sometimes, to meet oneself anew. Grace, an elementary school teacher, spends years wondering if her work means enough. She dreams of joining an education program in South America, unsure if she will thrive. Once she arrives in Argentina, every new friendship and lesson plan becomes a step toward rediscovering why she started teaching at all. This kind of renewal is rarely possible within the confines of a life fully mapped. The chance to grow through fresh adversity infuses daily existence with excitement. Spontaneity returns, and overcoming even small hurdles can offer powerful feelings of achievement.

The drive to explore other worlds goes beyond vague restlessness. Interest in other cultures and histories ignites curiosity and resilience. When Raheem moves to Seoul for a job, he is enthralled by both the language and the unwritten rules that govern everyday interactions. During his first Chuseok celebration, he learns the story behind each dish and why elders are honored first. Each encounter prompts him to question assumptions from his upbringing, forcing him to adjust, adapt, and sometimes laugh at his mistakes. Rather than simply being entertained, expats like Raheem find that immersion in new traditions becomes its own kind of education, creating space for transformation. Cultural curiosity provides both motive and the tools required to weather early challenges.

New skills, unexpected friendships, and expanded worldviews often emerge from the pursuit of international opportunities, both personal and professional. Consider Priya, a marketing manager who accepts a position in Berlin after years in Mumbai. The shift brings more than career advancement. Working alongside colleagues with different backgrounds, she develops patience and flexibility, learning to thrive despite language barriers and unfamiliar workplace dynamics. Over time, she builds a global network, discovers new methods for creative problem solving, and achieves a confidence unimagined in her previous role. This kind of growth is not only theoretical; it is rooted in practice, challenge, and the tangible rewards of risk.

Early experiences abroad are rarely smooth. Homesickness can strike unexpectedly, no matter how prepared one feels. Longing for familiar food, conversations, or familiar sights creeps in during moments of stillness. Feeling out of place at grocery stores or celebrations is universal. Maintaining regular contact with friends and relatives helps ground new expats. Scheduling weekly calls can create much-needed stability. Participating in local events or classes offers opportunities to build new bonds and invest emotionally in the new place. Creating daily routines—morning jogs, favorite markets, even weekly movie nights—helps bridge the gap between old life and new.

Self-doubt can shadow the first months. Old anxieties rear up: Was this a mistake? Will I ever fit in? Writing down the reasons for moving and reading them during moments of uncertainty can remind new arrivals of their original motivations. Finding community among fellow expats can offer camaraderie and practical advice. Mindfulness and positive affirmations help to quiet the critical voices and focus on achievements, no matter how small. Each day brings unmistakable evidence of resilience, from navigating the transit system to ordering dinner in a new language.

Initial challenges mark the start of a larger transformation. Facing homesickness and self-doubt requires inner strength and practical effort. Slowly, routines develop, confidence grows, and the once-daunting unknown becomes just another part of daily life. With each hurdle crossed, a deeper sense of possibility begins to take root.

## Embracing Uncertainty and Taking Action: Building Resilience and Practical Foundations

Longstanding routines and support systems rarely move with you. The old safety nets—loved ones a short drive away, a favored coffee shop, the mutual understanding of neighbors—drift into memory the moment you arrive in a foreign country. This shift demands that new expats figure out how to build again from the ground up, often with no familiar anchors. The absence of known networks is unsettling, yet it is also a powerful teacher. Discovering how to forge new circles means taking small but steady steps: finding community notice boards, searching out local interest groups, and saying yes to social invitations, even if discomfort comes along. People often join language exchange groups or attend workshops for hobbies, like painting or dance, both to learn and to connect. Even introducing yourself to neighbors, inviting them for tea, or joining nearby fitness classes offers footholds for new friendships. These small investments gradually take root, helping the unfamiliar begin to feel more like home.

Building self-reliance becomes essential when old routines don't fit. Everyday challenges—finding the local pharmacy, navigating grocery stores, reading signs—shift from small tasks to mini-victories. Each solution adds a layer of confidence and resilience. Establishing a personal routine grounds you. Start by setting daily touchstones, such as a morning walk, journaling, or an evening meal at the same time. These steady points become lifelines when other parts of life feel turbulent.

## Embracing Uncertainty and Growing Through Change

Uncertainty sits at the core of any international move, amplifying the sense of vulnerability that comes from leaving the known behind. Instead of fighting it, embrace uncertainty as an ally. See each day not as a test, but as an open question. This mindset turns moments of doubt into chances for adaptation and creativity. When an expat faces unexpected language barriers at the post office or must adjust when apartments fall through, a flexible attitude ensures these moments serve as growth rather than setbacks.

A curious approach leads to surprising advantages. Trying unfamiliar foods at a street market, signing up for a pottery class in an unknown neighborhood, or even navigating local festivals opens up gateways to self-discovery and expanded worldviews. By leaning into change and experimenting with new skills, expats not only manage unfamiliarity but also inoculate themselves against feeling helpless. Over time, resilience grows from every small risk and each challenge met.

## Laying the Practical Groundwork: Paperwork and Logistical Stability

Understanding and managing documentation is essential for security and peace of mind. Begin research well before departure. Identify all necessary paperwork—visa applications, residency permits, health insurance documents. Make comprehensive checklists, and categorize required documents by urgency and renewal dates. Create digital backups of every important document, store them securely in the cloud, and keep printed copies in a secure folder. Leverage the resources of local consulates and embassies for accurate instructions, and reach out to expat forums where others share expertise about recent policy changes or successful filing strategies. When in doubt, consult with local legal advisors to avoid pitfalls from misfiling or lapses in registration.

## Housing Tactics for a Smooth Landing

The search for housing is rarely straightforward. Start with flexible arrangements such as short-term rentals through trusted platforms, serviced apartments, or recommendations from established expat communities. These options buy time and reduce the pressure to sign unfamiliar long-term contracts. Carefully scrutinize rental agreements for details on deposits, utilities, and cancellation terms. Seek out reviews or firsthand testimonials to confirm safety and suitability. An expat might choose a month-to-month sublet as a low-risk first step, giving space to learn neighborhoods before settling long-term.

## Managing Money and Setting Financial Boundaries

Adapting to a new economic environment requires vigilance. Calculate an initial budget based on estimated daily expenses, rent, and transportation. Track every expense from day one, using local budgeting apps that convert currencies in real-time. Consider opening an account with a local bank, especially if your stay is more than a few months. Compare banking app features to find those with low international transaction fees and easy mobile access. Monitor price changes on essentials, from groceries to transit fares, and identify ways to economize—such as local discount cards or by frequenting affordable markets. Practical vigilance brings a sense of control amid fluctuating costs.

## Navigating Transport and Building Freedom of Movement

Mobility unlocks independence. Spend the first weeks studying public transportation maps, testing routes to grocery stores, workplaces, and social venues. Download robust transit apps—many include English options with real-time updates. Observe local commuting rhythms to avoid rush hour or to find the safest paths home. Firsthand exploration, like riding buses along their full route or mapping out walking distances, offers grounding familiarity. Stories of expats discovering a favorite tram line or learning which stations sell affordable monthly passes show that mastering transport streams daily life toward routine and predictability.

Even with strong routines, frustrations will arise. Rigid plans may unravel, and early victories can be offset by fresh hurdles—confusing bureaucracies, sudden loneliness, or cultural missteps. Normalizing these setbacks prepares you to cope and adjust, forging onward with greater resilience as the journey continues into the depths of the un-known.

## Overcoming Early Setbacks: Solutions for Common Expat Challenges

When the suitcase is finally unpacked and the first morning in a strange country dawns, discomfort slips in before breakfast. The city hums with unfamiliar sounds, shopkeepers speak in rapid syllables that tangle the tongue, and the street maps feel like abstract art. Initial adaptation means more than navigating different currency or buying groceries; it demands a bruising kind of resilience and a willingness to stand exposed, uncertain but eager to learn.

Language difficulties are the earliest and often the sharpest thorns. Words once instinctive become slippery and unreliable. An expatriate spends minutes rehearsing a simple request for coffee, only to blurt it out with a comical twist at the counter. The barista smiles and corrects the order, perhaps with an amused shake of the head. These moments are humbling, but each one offers a lesson. The mechanism at work here is psychological habituation—the more an adult will-ingly subjects themselves to these awkward stumbles, the less acute their anxiety becomes. Deliberate mistakes, paired with a readiness to laugh at oneself, create space for connection. A new arrival who mis-pronounces a local idiom and laughs alongside the shop owner isn't just learning vocabulary; they are practicing vulnerability. This open, humorous approach encourages others to help, accelerating both trust and language acquisition.

Social isolation drifts in almost silently. The new city is thick with faces and conversations, yet at night the flat is quiet and the echo of home grows louder. Making friends as an adult, especially in a culture where one did not grow up, feels like picking a lock with cold fingers. A practical path out of this loneliness is intentional partici-pation. Instead of waiting to be included, expats benefit when they seek out regular events. For example, joining a local hiking group or language exchange meetup creates shared ground where relationships can root. Volunteering is especially powerful, offering a role and a set of responsibilities that signal trust to others. Each new acquaintance, every shared coffee, chips away at isolation. Social connection is not the result of a single lucky encounter but of sustained, small efforts that nudge at loneliness until it relents.

Bureaucracy forms an obstacle course with rules printed only in the local language and no clear instructions. Registering with city au-thorities, finding the right residence permit, or visiting the doctor for the first time can become odysseys that test both patience and prob-lem-solving skills. Take, for instance, an expat who waits at a govern-ment office for hours, only to discover a forgotten document means starting over tomorrow. Emotional exhaustion rises alongside practi-cal frustration. The most effective strategy here combines preparation, documentation, and asking for guidance. Organizing all paperwork in a dedicated folder, requesting written step-by-step directions from others who have succeeded, and bringing a bilingual friend or inter-preter can transform a daunting task into a manageable one. Rather than seeing bureaucratic battles as defeats, many long-term expats find meaning in the skills they develop: patience, negotiation, and the quiet pride of cracking the system at last. Each paper stamped is a victory, a tangible sign of progress.

Cultural disorientation weaves through every other challenge, appearing in small, persistent ways—a misunderstood joke at dinner, food that tastes foreign, or an unspoken rule about queuing that derails a morning commute. The mind tires easily under these pressures, and burnout feels closer than expected. Self-care provides guardrails. Recognizing stress signals—trouble sleeping, irritability, or persistent fatigue—allows adults to pause and recalibrate. A structured routine, familiar comforts like cooking a meal from home, and celebrating every minor success help restore energy and resolve. Marking the moment when a local greengrocer remembers your name, or when you finally use the perfect phrase in conversation, matters. These benchmarks do not erase the sense of alienation overnight, but they ground a person in the reality of forward motion.

Learning to endure and overcome these setbacks builds far more than logistical competence. Confidence grows from the willingness to stumble and try again. Mistakes in grammar or missteps in social etiquette become proof of perseverance, not failure. The rhythms of the new city begin to sync with one's pulse. Eventually, there are fewer mistakes, more inside jokes, and the knowledge that difficulty signals nothing more than the edge of growth. Each challenge—language, isolation, bureaucracy, and culture shock—reveals a lesson in self-acceptance and adaptability. Progress is measured not just by adaptation, but by the quieter triumph of becoming at home in oneself, wherever life may land.

## Concluding Thoughts

Now that we have explored the emotional and practical journey of moving abroad—from understanding the deep motivations that spark change to navigating early setbacks and building new routines—prospective expats are better equipped to face the uncertainties ahead with resilience and purpose. Recognizing that challenges like language barriers, homesickness, and cultural confusion are not signs of failure but milestones in personal growth allows travelers to approach their new lives with patience and flexibility. By embracing both the discomfort and excitement of adaptation, individuals can transform unfamiliar places into true homes while discovering strengths they never knew they had. This chapter lays the foundation for a meaningful overseas experience, encouraging readers to move forward with confidence and curiosity on the path to self-discovery and belonging.

# Waves of Culture Shock: Sinking and Swimming

A djusting to life in a new culture often feels like navigating unpredictable waves—moments of excitement followed by stretches of confusion and isolation. These emotional highs and lows are a natural part of settling into unfamiliar surroundings, where everyday routines suddenly require new skills and perspectives. For many newcomers, the challenge lies not only in understanding a different language or customs but also in managing feelings of vulnerability and finding ways to connect with others despite cultural divides.

This chapter delves into the experience of culture shock, examining how individuals cope with emotional ups and downs, learn to interpret unspoken social cues, overcome language challenges, and build meaningful relationships in a foreign environment. Through shared stories and practical guidance, it offers insight into the complex process of adaptation and highlights strategies that help newcomers find balance and belonging amid change.

## Riding the Emotional Waves: Adjusting and Connecting Amid Culture Shock

Landing in a new homeland, many expats feel swept up in the joyful current of the honeymoon phase. Every sight seems vibrant, every sound musical, each taste a revelation. Small rituals—clapping on subways in Buenos Aires, afternoon tea in England, street hawkers braiding jasmine in Bangkok—spark delight with their unfamiliarity. Nadia, newly settled in Chile, found herself photographing every meal: pastel de choclo steaming beside strong coffee, vivid fruit smoothies, sweets dusted with cinnamon. She wondered if daily life could always feel this magical, feeling the country was tailor-made for her sense of adventure. These early days, while intoxicating, can also distort expectations. It's easy to idealize a place with fresh eyes, believing language barriers will dissolve, friendships will sprout overnight, and homesickness won't touch an open mind. Recognizing that the sparkle is both exhilarating and temporary arms newcomers with realism—the first step in weathering culture shock's inevitable waves.

Attitudes shift. Days instead of whirling with surprise, drag or stumble under the weight of disillusionment. The unfamiliar now feels inconvenient rather than charming. Grocery shopping becomes a minefield of unreadable labels. Social invitations become scarce when conversations falter, or polite smiles mask confusion over unspoken customs. Martin, a Canadian relocating to Osaka, tried to buy over-the-counter cold medicine but misread the instructions and returned home with something unhelpful and minty. His attempts to ask clerks for guidance only provoked blank looks. Afterward, he found himself missing the easygoing pharmacists back home, and feeling exposed by every misstep. At night, he missed friends who understood offhand jokes and struggled against loneliness that crept in at odd hours. These moments contain immense vulnerability. Yet the discomfort holds possibility—it exposes the gaps in understanding, true, but also demands that expats learn, adapt, and reach out. In these lows, resilience begins to form. By recognizing this is a phase, not a failing, newcomers can meet their struggles with more self-compassion. Keeping a journal, seeking out others' stories, and recalling small daily wins can help steady nerves and mark growth, even when progress is hard to see.

Adjustment arrives, not as a permanent plateau, but as a series of fits and starts—often two steps forward, one back. Good and bad days arrive without clear warning. Annette moved to southern Italy and, over months, picked up the rhythm of the local bus schedule and adopted the late-night dinner times. One evening she ordered food with the correct greeting without a tremor of nerves; another day she mispronounced a word and sparked laughter from a restaurant owner. Routines begin to solidify, but setbacks do too: a beloved café closes, seasonal festivals seem opaque, or a work meeting sparks uncertainty over etiquette. Accepting uneven progress is vital. It helps to celebrate moments of fluency, acknowledge setbacks with humor, and remember that belonging grows in small increments. Over time, what felt like daunting hurdles—learning nods of greeting, adapting to indirect feedback, or understanding work hierarchies—becomes part of daily life.

## List: Practices for Enduring Adjustment

- Join language groups or cultural clubs—even one meeting

can ground you in routine

- Schedule regular video calls with friends back home for emotional balance

- Allow for rest after demanding days; fatigue often heightens emotional dips

- Note customs that intrigue or challenge you

- Practice forgiveness when missteps occur

A strange relief can come in embracing not fitting in. Cultural awkwardness is a shared thread among global nomads, a gateway to insight and growth. At a networking event, Leila reached for a handshake while her Swiss colleague leaned in for a double cheek kiss; both paused mid-gesture, sparking nervous laughter. The miscue made her self-conscious, but it was also an opening. It prompted her to ask a local friend to explain unwritten rules. These stumbles, instead of pushing her away, encouraged her to ask questions, become flexible, and see others' perspectives with fresh empathy. Not fitting in is uncomfortable, but it is also where personal transformation begins. It pushes expats to stretch assumptions, listen deeply, and trust themselves to navigate uncertainty.

Over time, misunderstandings and hesitancy in cross-cultural relationships can give way to camaraderie. Consider the story of Amir and Simon, both teachers at an international school, who initially clashed over communication styles—Amir's indirectness and Simon's bluntness led to pointed silences and awkward lunches. Gradually, a shared passion for football emerged. Debates over teams replaced tense pauses; good-natured teasing bridged gaps. Through humor and curiosity, they learned to decode each other's intentions, developing trust that made difficult moments feel surmountable. A joke shared during a paperwork mix-up illuminated how humor itself could transcend language, and small efforts to understand each other seeded true friendship. Watching the pair review classroom plans—unspoken cues passing between them—revealed how slowly, through persistence and openness, deep connection becomes possible even in unfamiliar territory.

## Unwritten Rules: Navigating Social Codes with Confidence

Feeling uncertain or even awkward in a new place often comes from suddenly facing unfamiliar social rules. The first days or weeks in a different country can sharpen this realization. Gentle gestures or casual remarks that go unnoticed at home might spark confusion or draw puzzled looks abroad. The path through this maze starts with recognizing the central role that local etiquette plays in building relationships. Instead of treating these unwritten codes as obstacles, they can become a map for navigating through the unfamiliar social landscape.

Small details often matter the most. When greeting someone, a handshake may signal respect in Germany, while in Japan, bowing is the expected gesture. A kiss on the cheek may be common among friends in Argentina, but would feel out of place in many parts of the U.S. or East Asia. A traveler who extends a hand as a first approach in France, where a kiss on the cheeks is conventional, might notice a brief moment of hesitation, revealing that a misstep, however slight, has occurred. Even without words, reactions in posture or facial expression give valuable feedback on what is considered natural or acceptable.

Awareness of context gives important clues. Tone of voice, the formality of speech, or even the distance between people during a conversation often signal the right approach. Loud talking feels normal in some Mediterranean cultures, where warmth and expressiveness go hand-in-hand. In contrast, more reserved Scandinavian countries may view raised voices in public as impolite or even aggressive. Similarly, physical space varies greatly. Standing close during a conversation may create a sense of intimacy in Brazil but feel invasive in Japan.

Some missteps can lead to more than awkwardness. For example, in Thailand, touching someone's head, even affectionately, can be deeply disrespectful since the head is considered sacred. Conversely, placing your feet on a chair or desk—harmless in some Western countries—may offend in cultures where feet are considered dirty or lowly. Paying attention to the way locals move and behave during greetings, meals, and goodbyes often helps newcomers absorb these boundaries.

Social awareness extends into topics of conversation. In some countries, discussing work or salary openly builds rapport. In others, such questions are too forward, bordering on rude. Questions about age, marital status, or family life may be light and typical icebreakers in Korea or Turkey, while they could seem intrusive in the UK or the United States. In many cultures, religion and politics are sensitive issues—best avoided until one understands the group's comfort level. Observing what friends and colleagues freely talk about, and where they hesitate or change subject, helps guide newcomers on what is appropriate.

Practical steps for decoding these social codebooks begin with careful observation. Before joining a group conversation or making a joke, listening to rhythms and habits of local speech is revealing. Noticing who speaks first, how opinions are introduced, and how disagreements are handled plants a strong foundation for integration. A newcomer might watch in Spain how friends linger at the table, exchanging personal stories long after the meal is finished, understanding that shared time is valued more than punctuality. In contrast, in northern Europe or the U.S., meals may move briskly, and lingering can feel out of place or inconsiderate if it delays another scheduled activity.

Anecdotes from long-term expats often highlight early stumbles—from using first names too soon in a formal setting to showing up late for dinner in places where time is strictly observed. Such stories reveal how even seasoned travelers remain learners, needing to adjust their behaviors according to each new situation.

Mastering small talk marks a significant stage in cultural adaptation. Some societies, such as Australia or the U.K., prefer conversations gently propelled by humor or weather talk, keeping interactions light and non-intrusive. In contrast, in Russia or Argentina, conversations often venture into current events or personal opinions quickly, reflecting a comfort with deeper topics early in the relationship. Matching the local pace and topic of conversation shapes the impression newcomers make, sometimes opening doors to friendship, other times closing them if the codes go ignored.

Every step in decoding new social codes builds upon watching, listening, and modeling behavior after local friends and colleagues. When mistakes happen, adjusting with kindness towards oneself and a readiness to learn speaks volumes, often earning respect. Consistent observation not only prevents embarrassing moments but fosters an atmosphere of mutual understanding. As the world of social etiquette opens up, attention shifts naturally towards the subtler world of communication—where spoken and unspoken cues intertwine, and language itself becomes the next challenge to decipher.

## Language Barriers: Practical Strategies for Communication Beyond Words

Stepping into a world where gestures speak louder than words, many find themselves navigating puzzles only language can crack. At first, understanding the subtle cues in a market or a workplace—what tone signals respect, how a pause can mean disagreement—demands keen observation. But the sensation of standing outside a conversation intensifies whenever the spoken words themselves become foreign terrain.

The first days in a new country often feel like moving through fog. The buzz of conversation at a café blurs into noise. Ordering food, asking directions, or joining in small talk triggers anxiety, not from lack of intent, but from the weight of every unknown syllable. This is where language stops being invisible and transforms into a daily challenge.

Many adults struggle with the feeling of suddenly seeming young or incapable. People who once led meetings now find themselves fumbling to ask for simple things, slowed by the effort of recall and pronunciation. Beyond embarrassment, frustration simmers, especially as missed jokes or fast exchanges leave them outside of laughter or group decisions. Yet, there's a hidden key—a mindset shift made by those who eventually thrive: welcoming the role of beginner with curiosity rather than shame.

Children learn languages without worrying about perfection. They accept correction, laugh when words come out wrong, and enjoy the adventure. Adults, less practiced at being vulnerable, often resist this humility. Expats who give themselves permission to be playful, to laugh at mistakes, discover moments of warmth even in mishaps.

Mispronouncing a word in a shop can lead to shared laughter with the cashier, turning embarrassment into camaraderie.

## Embracing Growth Through Everyday Struggles

A digital nomad in Berlin, Aisha, remembers how her first attempts at German involved many awkward pauses and apologies in line at the bakery. Rather than shrinking away, she began to treat each small interaction as a language lesson. One stumbling phrase helped her discover the correct pronunciation from a patient vendor; another miscommunication gave her a story to share with expat friends. These tiny episodes, instead of building a wall of shame, formed stepping stones to confidence.

Technology offers a bridge across these gaps, with smartphones serving as instant translators and teachers. Translation apps unravel menus, directions, and even transit systems. Voice recognition helps with correct inflection. Platforms like Duolingo or Babbel build vocabulary bit by bit, creating pockets of progress while commuting or relaxing at home.

Yet, technology holds limits. Typed translations can oversimplify or muddle meaning, and dependence on screens may keep people distant from authentic conversation. Insights from seasoned language learners reveal the value of face-to-face practice. Joining a local language club, chatting with neighbors, or volunteering for community events gives lessons context and stakes. Struggles transform into memories, and fluency is shaped not just by knowing the right words, but by forgetting the fear of using the wrong ones.

## Harnessing the Power of the Unspoken

Words are not the only currency. Human connection often leans on a certain smile, a nod, the widening of eyes. In Tokyo's packed stations, a hesitant but earnest bow can speak volumes. In Latin America, a friendly wave or hug, timed just right, dissolves distance. Hand movements and facial expressions amplify spoken meaning or cushion misunderstandings.

Reading the local style of non-verbal expression becomes part of language learning. When words stumble, miming an action—pointing, demonstrating, showing photos—keeps communication flowing. Listening with the eyes as well as the ears helps catch subtleties: a friendly tone softening direct words, a frown signaling confusion. Expats who tune in to these nuances often earn greater trust, building bonds that words alone can't guarantee.

## Turning Misunderstandings Into Connection

No matter how diligent, misunderstandings lurk in every interaction. An American teacher in rural France once meant to compliment a parent's bread, but chose the wrong gender for the word, suggesting something quite unintended. The family's laughter, rather than coldness, created an opening for friendship. Shared apologies, mutual patience, and even gentle teasing remind everyone that learning together makes communities stronger.

Rather than dreading or hiding mistakes, learners who treat them as part of the experience invite conversation. Locals often respond with encouragement, advice, or their own stories of language mishaps. Each fresh error builds resilience and signals a willingness to participate in new worlds, turning loneliness into belonging and hesitation into growth. Lingering in the discomfort of not knowing finally gives way to the joy of small victories—a friendly nod, a shared laugh, and the steady arrival of confidence.

## Summary and Reflections

Now that we understand the emotional ups and downs, the importance of decoding social cues, and the challenges of language barriers, newcomers can approach culture shock with greater patience and confidence. Accepting that adjustment is a gradual process filled with both setbacks and breakthroughs allows expats to embrace their unique journey without harsh self-judgment. By staying curious, practicing kindness toward themselves, and seeking connection despite differences, they can transform moments of confusion into opportunities for growth and deeper relationships. With these insights, those living abroad are better equipped not only to survive culture shock but to thrive in their new communities, building a meaningful life enriched by diversity and resilience.

# Loss and Reinvention: Shedding the Old Self

"I never thought ordering a simple coffee could feel so complicated," Ana confessed, glancing around the bustling café in her new city. Back home, these small interactions were automatic, effortless moments woven into daily life. Now, each exchange felt like navigating a maze without a map—every word weighed, every gesture uncertain. The familiar rhythms she once took for granted seemed distant, as if she had slipped into a world where her old self no longer quite fit.

Ana's experience mirrors what many face when stepping into life abroad. Leaving behind known routines and identities, the everyday becomes a subtle challenge that stirs deeper questions about who we are beneath the surface. It is not just about learning a language or customs; it is about confronting the parts of ourselves shaped by place and habit, then deciding what to hold onto and what to release.

The process can be disorienting and at times painful, yet within that discomfort lies the opportunity for profound personal change.

This chapter explores the quiet transformation that emerges as the old self is shed to make way for a new, more adaptable identity. It delves into the emotional hurdles, the unexpected losses, and the psychological adjustments that often accompany expatriate life. Through stories of struggle and moments of insight, readers will find reflections that resonate with their own journeys and discover the value of embracing uncertainty as a space for growth. Here, amid unfamiliar surroundings, lies the potential to rebuild from within—helping individuals move toward resilience, self-awareness, and a lasting sense of well-being.

## Identity Reconstruction and Selective Letting Go: Redefining Who You Are and What You Keep

Landing in a new country often feels like stepping onto a stage without a script. Habits and identities shaped by the rhythms of home life are challenged immediately. Achievements that provided confidence and social recognition might seem invisible, if not irrelevant, when language or cultural cues differ. The experienced professional in their own country may struggle to open a bank account or even order lunch, as happened to a graphic designer who moved from New York to Tokyo. Accustomed to being praised for her fast-paced work and creativity, she found herself slowed down by basic language barriers, her professional self-image forced into the background as she relearned how to navigate daily life from scratch. Such experiences strip away assumptions about who we are, exposing the bare core of identity, untethered from old contexts.

In these moments, values and beliefs that once guided decisions come under scrutiny. Confronted by unfamiliar customs and social rules, expatriates regularly find themselves asking, "Why do I do things this way?" or "Is this value truly mine, or just inherited?" One American man in southern Spain faced a dilemma each afternoon when shops closed for siesta. Frustrated by the pause in productivity, he initially scoffed at the tradition. Only after conversations with local friends and time spent observing a culture that prized relaxation and communal meals did he recognize the virtue in slowing down. This realization shifted his beliefs about work and rest, prompting him to reconsider his tendency to prioritize constant productivity over mental well-being.

The day-to-day roles assumed in a new country expand further on this sense of dislocation while creating opportunities for personal growth. Taking responsibility for tasks usually outsourced to family, social networks, or institutional systems back home, such as navigating health care or advocating for oneself in bureaucratic encounters, builds resilience. A Canadian woman in Argentina become a translator not just of language but of cultural subtext for her expat friends. Stepping into this new responsibility helped her recognize capacities she never developed at home. Learning to communicate in another language transforms the way self-expression works, offering the challenge—and reward—of making mistakes in public, then seeing incremental progress. Each new role claimed abroad adds dimension to personal identity, enlarging the notion of self to include traits such as adaptability and openness.

The aching sense of loss that arises during the first months abroad—confusion, nostalgia, and disconnection—is hard to escape. These feelings can be harnessed, however, as pivot points rather than traps. A young teacher in rural Korea, struggling with intense homesickness, began writing nightly reflections about what she missed and why. Through this journaling practice, she started identifying sources of comfort she could build anew in her host country, such as cooking familiar foods or organizing small gatherings. This process transformed her confusion into a toolkit for personal reinvention. Trying to see unfamiliar situations as invitations to grow, rather than threats to stability, helps expatriates use disorientation as a springboard for proactive transformation.

Letting go of emotional baggage is crucial in these moments of transition. Holding onto resentment over lost status or roles weighs down the possibility of renewal. Many expatriates find they must mindfully release the urge to compare everything to life back home—or harbor fears about not fitting in. One French engineer in Singapore realized that constantly complaining about local bureaucracy created only distance between herself and her new colleagues. She decided to pause before venting, practicing curiosity and patience even when frustrated. This shift cleared the way for deeper relationships and emotional clarity.

Evaluating established habits is equally important. Some routines, such as weekly exercise or daily meditation, carry over and even help anchor a person. Others, like clinging to old meal times or always seeking familiar foods, may hamper integration. When a British expatriate in Vietnam found herself lonely every evening, she reflected on her habit of eating alone at home and began joining communal street dinners, discovering not only connection but a sense of adventure. By pausing to assess which habits support growth and which block it, expatriates free up mental space for new experiences.

Minimalism becomes more than just a trend as people abroad streamline both possessions and emotional clutter. Letting go of nonessential items before a big move illustrates how much lighter one feels physically and mentally. A young family in Portugal sold most of their belongings and packed only essentials, allowing them to move with flexibility and less worry. This intentional decluttering of both "stuff" and attachments makes it easier to adapt, focus, and build happiness in a changing environment.

A deliberate inventory of the past helps with adaptation. Expatriates who choose to preserve a favorite recipe, daily walk, or core value while consciously discarding others benefit from the comfort of continuity amid change. One Indian man in France kept his tradition of morning chai, which gave him stability, while letting go of rigid family mealtime expectations that clashed with his new reality. Such thoughtful selection supports emotional resilience and a sense of rootedness.

Uncertainty lingers, a subtle, questioning tension, while the boundaries between old and new selves remain blurred and not yet fully reconciled.

## Triggers and Trauma: Understanding Psychological Stressors and Coping Mechanisms Abroad

Examining the layers of personal habits and deep-seated values often draws awareness to a more subtle terrain: the emotional landscape shaped by years of patterns, beliefs, and unresolved experiences. After some time abroad, it is not uncommon for expats to discover that beneath shifts in outward behavior lies a field of psychological triggers and recurring emotional difficulties. These responses push and prod from within, influencing each day's sense of stability, comfort, and control, even as the conscious mind grapples with changes in culture or routine.

Psychological stress during expatriation often comes not just from visible obstacles, but from the hidden tension of dislocation. Day after day, there may be low-level anxiety triggered by feeling out of sync with the rhythms of an unfamiliar city, or the gnawing discomfort of navigating subtle yet persistent cultural misunderstandings. For example, a relocation professional accustomed to direct feedback in the workplace may find themselves overwhelmed or demoralized when colleagues in the host country communicate indirectly or avoid confrontation, leading to self-doubt and confusion. A digital nomad worrying about sudden illness in a place where both the language and healthcare protocols are foreign may experience panic in situations previously considered routine. These challenges can spark anxiety, mood swings, irritability, and, sometimes, a cascade of intrusive memories or flashbacks—symptoms reminiscent of trauma responses.

Cultural isolation can amplify these responses. The loss of familiar anchors—like a favorite café, dependable friendships, or the ease of expressing oneself fluently—can lead to withdrawal or a recurring sense of dread before social events. Over time, loneliness or frustration with ongoing language barriers might grow into a persistent low mood or a pattern of emotional outbursts over minor inconveniences.

## Recognizing Emotional Tripwires

Noticing these internal patterns as they emerge can allow for more effective self-care. Early warning signs may appear as nightly bouts of restlessness, a sudden heaviness before venturing into public spaces, or repeated tension in interactions with local customs. Tracking these patterns, perhaps by jotting down moods at various points in the day, illuminates moments when stress is at its highest. By paying attention to situations—such as the anticipation of making a phone call in another language, or the energy dip after a misunderstanding at a market—expats can begin to identify their emotional tripwires.

Detecting triggers early helps prevent escalation. When someone recognizes that going to crowded markets always creates a sense of panic, for example, they can prepare by allowing extra time, inviting a friend along, or building in a soothing routine afterward. Awareness of one's reactivity turns nebulous discomfort into something tangible, opening a space for intervention and self-compassion.

## Practical Tools for Grounding and Control

Therapeutic strategies for immediate support are most effective when clear, concrete, and easily adaptable. Grounding exercises bring attention back to the present body and moment, interrupting spirals of anxious thought or emotional flooding. Deep breathing—such as inhaling for four counts, holding for four, and exhaling for four—can be done quietly in a crowded train or while waiting for an appointment. Naming objects in sight or describing textures, temperatures, and sounds redirects the mind from internal distress to the outer senses. Even a routine as simple as feeling one's feet firmly on the ground while pressing toes against the insoles brings a sense of safety and control when panic threatens to take hold.

These strategies are most useful when practiced during calm moments and then intentionally recalled when distress creeps in. A personalized "grounding script" written in a notebook or phone, or a list of sensory activities, can serve as a lifeline when emotions begin to surge. With time, such routines create a sense of agency, encouraging resilience by teaching the nervous system how to return to balance.

## Navigating Mental Health Support Abroad

Accessing professional support has its own set of complications for expatriates. Local stigma against mental health issues, lack of fluency in the host country's language, or confusion about healthcare logistics can make reaching out daunting. Finding counselors or therapists with cross-cultural understanding improves communication and increases trust. Expats might connect with local support groups for shared experience or use online therapy platforms that offer sessions in a preferred language. Researching in advance where and how mental healthcare can be accessed—or asking other expats about their experiences—lowers barriers to seeking help when the need arises.

## Rewriting the Personal Narrative

Healing also comes from the process of reclaiming agency over one's story. Reflective journaling—especially written soon after challenging events—allows for emotional processing in private. Writing about misunderstandings at work or a difficult hospital visit, followed by reframing what those struggles reveal about personal strength or adaptability, turns raw emotion into self-knowledge. Listing new skills or moments of resilience unearthed during hardship builds a library of inner resources to draw from in tougher times. This practice reduces internal shame, creates a more empowered self-concept, and highlights progress that might otherwise go unrecognized.

In combination, early trigger recognition, accessible coping tools, and the ongoing work of narrative healing create a web of support that helps individuals move from overwhelmed to adaptive. As expats deepen these skills, emotional flexibility becomes a hallmark of their experience—gently shaping a path toward sustained wellbeing and an openness to the complex joys of an unfamiliar life. The benefits of this psychological resilience continue to unfold, quietly guiding the way toward longer-lasting happiness and adaptation.

## Liberation Through Change: The Power and Long-Term Impact of Adaptation

Greater awareness of emotions lays the foundation for transformative adaptation. Living abroad brings unfamiliar stressors that require more than simply enduring discomfort; they invite a deeper exploration of self. For many, adjustment begins with recognizing emotional patterns—anxiety at crowded markets, uncertainty when misunderstood, or frustration over differing social norms. Each emotional cue signals an opportunity for intentional change. Rather than ignoring these feelings, expatriates who build internal strength by acknowledging discomfort find themselves equipped for real growth. When moods are tracked and understood, it becomes easier to pinpoint triggers and respond thoughtfully, not reactively.

Adaptable thinking is the anchor point for sustained happiness in unfamiliar environments. Those who consciously shape their mindset approach new cultures with curiosity, not suspicion. For example, a newcomer might struggle with the overwhelming array of choices at a local bazaar. Instead of retreating, choosing to see confusion as part of the adventure makes a vital difference. Viewing mistakes through a lens of learning, such as mispronouncing phrases or missing social cues, transforms setbacks into catalysts for resilience. Each minor mishap becomes proof that growth is taking place, rather than evidence of failure.

### Practical Examples of Openness and Learning

Adopting openness in daily life has real consequences. Consider an expatriate who attempts to order coffee in a new language and receives an unexpected dish instead. By reframing the miscommunication as a shared moment of humor or as a step toward improvement, stress dissolves and connection flourishes. The effort itself becomes a small celebration; every attempt chips away at the fear of embarrassment.

Another illustration emerges on public transportation. Missing the correct stop can evoke panic, but adaptable thinkers quickly shift perspective. Getting lost opens up hidden corners of a city and provides memorable stories to share. With patience and a sense of humor, these experiences foster lasting flexibility and reduce future anxiety.

Positive reframing is a habit that grows stronger with use. An unsuccessful job search may initially feel like rejection, but over time, noticing even small improvements—better interview skills, expanded vocabulary, or growing professional networks—invites optimism. The practice of finding silver linings builds a pattern of resilience that equips expatriates to weather bigger storms.

## Celebrating Small Wins and Building Confidence

Savoring incremental victories has a powerful effect. Memorizing a handful of directions, making a local acquaintance, or receiving a genuine smile in a new neighborhood brings a sense of progress that is both motivating and affirming. When each achievement is noted, however small, the broader journey feels less daunting.

One practical way to encourage this mindset is to keep a daily log of "firsts," recording even the kind of accomplishment that initially seems insignificant. The act of writing down small milestones, such as managing a solo grocery trip or holding a brief conversation, creates a visible record of growth. This process boosts confidence and makes hurdles feel less intimidating. Progress becomes tangible, reminding individuals that personal change does not happen in giant leaps but in everyday steps taken with intention.

## Embracing Flexibility as a Lasting Advantage

Remaining open in the face of difference is an essential strength for expatriates. Customs and expectations vary widely, so rigid adherence to old ways often leads to frustration. Instead, flexible attitudes—whether adjusting to unfamiliar greetings, rethinking time management, or adapting to less direct communication styles—deepen creativity and problem solving. For instance, joining community activities that are not immediately comfortable, such as neighborhood festivals or holiday celebrations, expands horizons and fosters belonging.

To develop new flexibility, expatriates can try saying yes to invitations they might initially decline, ask questions rather than making assumptions, and resist the urge to compare new customs to old ones. With each conscious choice to adapt, relationships grow richer and connections feel more meaningful.

## The Enduring Power of Adaptation

Long-term adaptation does more than smooth daily challenges; it shapes a compassionate and informed worldview. Over time, those who repeatedly stretch their perspectives find themselves able to relate to people from all walks of life. Witnessing and accepting difference makes empathy second nature. The continuous habit of learning, unlearning, and relearning leads to lasting self-knowledge.

This process of becoming—reinforced by small victories, flexible thinking, and emotional awareness—transforms not only the expatriate experience but the person living it. The joy and resilience that result from ongoing adaptation last well beyond the excitement of novelty. They become a foundation for happiness that endures, rooted in the discovery that growth and fulfillment are always possible, wherever home may be.

## Concluding Thoughts

Now that we understand how expatriate life challenges us to rethink who we are, confront hidden emotional stresses, and develop flexibility, we can approach this journey with greater awareness and intention. Embracing the process of letting go—of old habits, familiar comforts, and limiting beliefs—opens the door to building resilience and new strengths. By recognizing and managing psychological triggers, practicing practical coping tools, and celebrating small progress, expats gain valuable skills for lasting well-being. Looking ahead, adopting an open mindset and welcoming change not only helps us navigate daily uncertainties but also fosters deeper empathy and personal growth. With these insights and strategies, those living abroad can transform challenges into opportunities, creating a more adaptable and fulfilling life wherever they choose to call home.

# Routines Remade: Building Life, Day by Day

Salma's eyes flutter open to the soft glow of morning light spilling over her unfamiliar studio apartment in Prague. She moves through a sequence of small, deliberate actions—breathing deeply, sipping water, jotting down thoughts—that feel like lifelines in a world that often feels unpredictable and strange. Nearby, Marco sets his phone timer, carving out precious pockets of focused work between moments of uncertainty in Tokyo. Léa finds comfort in organizing just one corner of her Moroccan kitchen, while Lydia creates personal boundaries around a cluttered desk in Seoul to preserve her energy. These fragments of daily life reveal a shared struggle: how to rebuild stability when everything else feels uncertain.

Adjusting to new surroundings means more than just managing tasks; it is about weaving together routines that protect well-being, sustain motivation, and nurture a sense of belonging. From reinventing self-care practices with limited resources, to translating professional skills into unfamiliar work cultures, to seeking meaningful ways to engage beyond the workplace, expats face layered challenges as they shape their lives abroad. The quiet strength found in these efforts rarely makes headlines, but it lays the groundwork for resilience and growth amid change.

Each day abroad unfolds not only in response to external demands but through intentional rhythms crafted by individuals striving to find balance. Whether navigating local markets or mastering a foreign language, setting boundaries or embracing novelty, these routines form the scaffolding that supports emotional and practical survival. Without them, the strain of cultural shifts and logistical hurdles can become overwhelming.

Through stories of real people adapting and redefining their days, this chapter invites reflection on how routine acts serve as anchors in shifting landscapes. It reveals the subtle ways that rebuilding daily life—step by step, moment by moment—becomes a powerful act of reinvention, offering insight and validation to those embarking on or dreaming of a life away from home.

## Establishing Stability and Self-Care in Unfamiliar Environments

Salma wakes in a small studio in Prague, sunlight stretching across a plain white duvet. Even before her eyes open fully, she follows a familiar routine—a few deep breaths in silence, a glass of water on the bedside table, and a short meditative journal session. Consistent morning rituals like these offer more than simple tasks; they create anchors. The predictability signals the mind that some things remain steady, regardless of what happens outside. Salma adapts her morning by including a new Czech herbal tea recommended by her neighbor, finding calm in both an old habit and a local influence. The blend of the familiar with something new quietly reassures her, showing that adapting a morning routine to personal tastes and surroundings can build emotional strength in unsettled times.

The stability gained from these rituals does not erase daily uncertainty. Many expats find it hard to predict what challenges a day might bring, from language mix-ups to unfamiliar bureaucracy. Flexible time management becomes crucial for keeping overwhelm at bay. Consider Marco, who relies on his phone's timer to carve out small work blocks in his Tokyo apartment. He sets a 40-minute focus period to draft a report, knowing that he will join new friends for a spontaneous ramen outing afterward. This simple use of technology brings a sense of order and accomplishment, even as he leaves room for surprises that make living abroad so dynamic. By breaking larger tasks into sections on a paper planner or a digital list, expats like Marco can adjust as needed while still progressing toward their goals.

Small, clear achievements fuel motivation in a life that feels like it's built on moving sand. Breaking down long-term objectives into mini-goals makes elusive ambitions manageable and visible. Léa, teaching English in Morocco, decides to organize her kitchen in one afternoon rather than tackling her entire apartment at once. The satisfaction of seeing a tidier, functional kitchen brings her a quiet confidence and a reason to celebrate—maybe by preparing a simple tagine with her new local spices. Completing and marking off these micro-goals, whether mastering a few new phrases or arranging a workspace, builds positive momentum. They also allow for regular, satisfying victories, essential for emotional well-being when external circumstances remain unpredictable.

Physical and emotional safe spaces stand as invisible scaffolding in unfamiliar environments. A small shelf with Spanish novels, a framed photo of a loved one, or the scent of lavender oil can turn a corner of a room into a personal haven. Lydia, who recently moved to Seoul, designates her desk as a work-only zone. She keeps her favorite mug and a small houseplant nearby, enforcing the boundary that emails and paperwork stay contained to those few square feet. This clear division of space preserves her energy and creates a buffer between external chaos and internal calm. Dedicating time for undisturbed relaxation in these safe spots, even for just thirty minutes in the evening, reinforces their protective quality.

Self-care underpins each day, demanding creativity and flexibility, especially when essentials look different abroad. Nutrition evolves through curiosity and willingness to adapt. Sam, who has never shopped outside major supermarkets, discovers comfort in a bustling Vietnamese produce market, learning the names of vegetables by sight and taste. He reinvents classic comfort meals using steamed local greens and new spices, cooking batches in a rented kitchenette when possible. For those with limited cooking options, even assembling a nourishing snack plate from market-fresh ingredients can provide both nutrition and emotional stability. Fitness, too, adapts to new realities—bodyweight routines in small spaces, brisk walks in unfamiliar neighborhoods, or practicing dance from an online class when the gym is unavailable. Enjoyable activities make movement feel like celebration, not obligation, which encourages consistency and uplifts the spirit.

Adapting sleep habits requires awareness and experimentation. Unfamiliar noises, new time zones, or different climates all threaten rest. Effective solutions include blackout curtains to block the early morning sun, earplugs for city traffic, or smartphone apps that play gentle rain sounds. Establishing a pre-sleep routine, such as reading for twenty minutes or writing down tomorrow's concerns, helps cue the body to wind down, signaling safety and rest despite a shifting environment.

Healthcare navigation, while intimidating, is essential to both peace of mind and resilience. Learning key medical phrases in the local language and compiling a short list of nearby clinics or emergency contacts transforms confusion into preparedness. Seeking out a local practitioner for a casual consultation builds trust before emergencies strike. Proactively managing prescriptions or scheduling regular checkups demonstrates respect for one's well-being and reduces the anxiety of the unknown.

Strong daily routines form the cornerstone for building a grounded, fulfilling life abroad. Once stability is woven into the fabric of daily living, expats can confidently bring that stability into new workplaces and professional challenges, ready to embrace opportunities with steady roots and renewed energy.

## Work Abroad: Carving a Professional Identity

The quiet routines carved out in a new country—morning exercise, healthy meals, moments set aside for self-care—do much more than offer stability. These habits build the steady confidence needed to step out into unfamiliar workplaces and evolving career landscapes. The wholeness found in daily rituals turns into a quiet self-assurance, helping people to carry their professional identities with them even as everything changes. With a settled heart and mind, the next step becomes finding ways to adapt and flourish at work.

Translating previous work experience requires a thoughtful look at the skills gained before, then considering how they make sense in an entirely different setting. Some abilities, like clear communication, adaptability, or project management, transcend specific industries and cultures. For instance, an engineer who led international projects back home will find that experience valuable. But to show this, they might need to describe familiar duties in new terms, highlighting how technical knowledge and teamwork can solve problems in any country. A teacher from one education system might focus on classroom management, creativity, or conflict resolution, which have value anywhere children gather to learn.

Updating resumes and portfolios forms a substantial part of this task. Every country has its expectations—some favor detailed work histories; others want a concise, streamlined summary. A professional moving from the U.S. to Germany, for example, discovers the importance of including a full education history and even a photo, while someone heading to the UK might place greater emphasis on relevant skills and voluntary experience. Along with these formal elements, demonstrating cultural awareness can help. Small adjustments—adjusting spellings, learning the local terminology, even switching from a functional to a chronological resume format—can signal that someone understands the customs of their new home.

Flexibility becomes essential as roles blur and change. Industries may expect different sets of responsibilities or demand a broader set of tasks than before. Imagine a marketing specialist who arrives in Southeast Asia. The job might call for involvement in community outreach, social media, and translation work, not only campaign strategy. By approaching each new responsibility with curiosity instead of hesitation, expats find themselves growing into more versatile professionals. Likewise, readiness to accept lateral or contract work—stepping stones in a wider journey—can become a source of pride rather than anxiety.

Navigating local workplace culture adds a layer of challenge and possibility. The same words or gestures that worked back home may seem confusing or even impolite in a new environment. In Japan, for example, deference to seniority and indirect communication is valued. Sharing one's opinion too openly in a meeting might be misinterpreted as disrespect. Meanwhile, a Swedish company's office may be characterized by informality, with open discussion and flat management hierarchies. Misunderstandings can be subtle: a colleague who says "maybe" might really mean "no," and a manager who never openly criticizes may expect employees to read between the lines.

To move through these moments gracefully, learning to observe first and ask questions often leads to understanding. Noticing how meetings are run—are they formal with strict agendas, or more casual discussions?—offers valuable clues. Marking local holidays in one's calendar, trying traditional foods with coworkers, or simply taking the time to greet colleagues in the local language all help to nurture goodwill. Listening carefully, following up privately for clarification, and occasionally seeking feedback reveal areas for growth while building trust over time.

The boundaries between remote and on-site work have blurred, presenting unique dilemmas for expats. Remote positions allow an engineer to keep contributing to their U.S.-based team while living in Spain, maintaining professional ties and a sense of continuity. The downside is feeling disconnected from the local community, missing chances to practice the language, or feeling adrift during local holidays. On-site work rewards immersion. Joining a French design studio or teaching at a Korean school offers daily language practice, cultural insights, and faster integration. Yet, it demands greater energy and flexibility during the adjustment period. Deciding between the two often depends on personal goals—whether one craves global connection or a strong local network, and how much risk or change feels reasonable at the time.

Professional confidence builds fastest with strong communication. Learning sector-specific vocabulary is crucial. Language courses aimed at doctors, engineers, or teachers meet this need, but real progress comes from regular use: participating in local association meetings, seeking mentorship from trusted colleagues, or even practicing small talk during coffee breaks. Every conversation, however brief, is a chance to absorb cultural cues, improve pronunciation, and uncover unspoken rules.

Gradually, the rhythms of professional and daily life blend together, offering room for something deeper—forming friendships, joining community groups, or volunteering. Through these moments, expats find that work no longer stands apart, but acts as a stepping stone to new forms of belonging and personal growth.

## Making Meaningful Days: Purposeful Engagement and Integration

Professional identity can become a foundation for daily rhythms, yet most expats soon realize a full and satisfying life means seeking purpose outside office walls. Days stretch open beyond tasks on the job, creating space to craft new routines and find personal fulfillment away from work. Many newcomers experience a sense of emptiness at first, but the canvas of free time becomes a rare chance to explore latent interests and rediscover joy in unexpected places.

The discovery of meaningful activities starts with an open mind. Newcomers often benefit from surveying the community for local clubs, gatherings, or shared-interest groups. Encountering a local running club or community choir might seem intimidating at first, but participation often leads to fast friendships and a sense of shared purpose. Someone with a longstanding love for cooking can join a neighborhood cooking class, where learning to prepare regional dishes offers not only pleasure but also the chance to interact with locals. Hobbyists in art or music can look for collaborative spaces that blend their interests with traditional art forms. A painter new to Kyoto, for example, might find fulfillment in adapting watercolor techniques to incorporate Japanese brushwork, guided by local instructors or peers.

## Discovering Local Passions

Nurturing fulfillment begins with small steps. Exploring community noticeboards, online groups, or even simple conversations at a café might reveal weekly knitting circles, book clubs, or neighborhood markets. These ventures often foster genuine connections. Merging personal interests with local customs, such as practicing yoga amidst ancient temple gardens or picking up dance movements unique to a region, creates powerful sensory memories. The process strengthens attachment to place and to people, making everyday routines more vibrant and meaningful.

Some expats are drawn to festivals or local holiday observances, which reveal traditions and open doors to seasonal pastimes. Joining a group to make holiday lanterns or participating in a riverside picnic can introduce newcomers to customs that foster friendship and a sense of belonging. Adjusting existing hobbies or discovering new ones infuses routine with enthusiasm and bridges cultural distances.

## Ongoing Learning as a Bridge

Growth and adaptation often hinge on continuous learning. Enrolling in a language course does more than teach vocabulary; it
grounds newcomers in the rhythm and nuance of daily exchange.
Someone attending evening French lessons in Paris might soon gain
enough confidence to order at local markets or chat with neighbors, making daily life less daunting. Skill-based workshops also offer
structure and prosperity. Weekend ceramics sessions or contemporary
dance classes anchor the calendar with positive anticipation, while
a short course in local business law or digital marketing provides a
pathway to greater competence and employability.

Learning makes entry into a new society feel more attainable. Pur-
suing professional certifications recognized in the new country, such
as first aid or child care, both expands career options and builds a
broader social network. Even small achievements—successfully greeting a neighbor in the local language or baking bread using a traditional
recipe—spark pride and a sense of progress.

## Volunteerism and Community Impact

Volunteering offers a unique opportunity for connection and personal
renewal. Committing to a few hours each week at a food bank or
animal shelter places expats side by side with locals, working toward
shared goals. Mentoring other newcomers can turn personal experience into a bridge of support and understanding, while environmental
clean-ups or community gardening projects foster pride in a shared
home and cultivate deep-rooted relationships. Each effort brings expats into new circles, encourages empathy, and rewards them with
gratitude and camaraderie that echo beyond immediate tasks.

Service provides a sense of purpose that counteracts the isolation
of adjusting to a new country. Giving back not only shapes the com-

munity but also reinforces self-worth, making every act, from tutoring children to joining a local recycling initiative, deeply valuable.

## Finding Fulfillment Through Novelty

Every expat faces moments of restlessness, when routines grow dull and energy wanes. Seeking novelty energizes these quieter moments and deepens appreciation for the host culture. Tasting street foods never seen before, wandering side streets to uncover hidden murals, or trying one's hand at basket weaving delivers bursts of discovery and excitement. Curiosity, when allowed to guide daily life, unlocks creativity and builds resilience, especially during periods when homesickness or culture shock threaten to overwhelm.

Balancing comforting routines with regular encounters of the new keeps days textured with meaning. Simple habits—such as keeping a curiosity journal or scheduling a "new experience day" each week—help maintain momentum. By blending freshness and familiarity, expats craft a steady sense of belonging rooted in constant growth. Each intentional choice and activity becomes a stepping stone toward a rich, self-directed life, anchored firmly in both local culture and enduring personal interests.

## Bringing It All Together

Now that we understand how establishing stable routines, adapting self-care, reshaping professional identities, and engaging meaningfully in new environments help create a grounded life abroad, expats can approach their transition with greater confidence and clarity. By blending familiar habits with local customs, breaking goals into manageable steps, and remaining open to learning and connection, newcomers lay the foundation for resilience and growth. This chapter's insights offer practical tools and inspiration to transform uncertainty into opportunity, enabling each individual to build a fulfilling daily life that supports both personal well-being and professional success in unfamiliar surroundings.

# Coping Mechanisms: Weathering the Emotional Storms

**M**aria stood frozen in the crowded Berlin bakery, struggling to understand the clerk's repeated question. Her cheeks flushed with embarrassment as negative thoughts swirled—"I'm not fitting in," "I'll never get this right." Moments like these are familiar for many living far from home, where everyday interactions can feel overwhelming and isolating. The emotional challenges of adapting to a new culture often go unnoticed until they build into exhaustion or withdrawal. This chapter delves into the subtle ways expats experience and respond to stress abroad, exploring how small shifts in mindset and daily habits can quietly support emotional strength amid uncertainty. It invites readers to understand the common struggles that come with living overseas and to consider practical approaches to staying resilient when life feels unsettled.

## Building Psychological Resilience and Recognizing Early Burnout Signs

A new arrival in Berlin stands at the bakery counter, tongue-tied, as the clerk frowns and impatiently repeats the question. Scenarios like these awaken a flood of negative self-talk—automatic thoughts insisting, "I'm failing at this," or "I'll never be good enough here." But resilience grows from challenging these harsh internal commentaries. Whenever a mistake or misunderstanding strikes, mentally pausing is critical. Start by noticing the negative thought. Admit its presence rather than letting it cycle unchallenged. Then, scrutinize its accuracy: Is it fair to leap to "I'm hopeless" after a single awkward exchange? Replace that script. Instead of "I always mess things up," try, "Learning a language includes moments of confusion. Each attempt makes tomorrow smoother." This approach transforms fleeting self-doubt into gentle, persistent encouragement.

### Exercise: Rewriting Self-Talk

1. When a setback or stressful moment happens, write down your first thought.

2. Ask: "Is this absolutely true? What evidence do I have?"

3. Generate an alternative statement. Aim for something supportive and realistic, like "I am persistent, and this is just one part of my adaptation."

4. Review your reworded statement in the evening. Notice patterns. Gradually, these revised narratives replace old ones.

After reframing inner monologues, attention often shifts outward—to the unpredictable, sometimes bewildering fabric of daily life abroad. Emotional rigidity—clinging to the same interpretations or routines—can leave expats feeling stuck when customs, schedules, or systems misfire. Cultivating cognitive flexibility encourages adaptability, turning missteps into manageable puzzles instead of crises.

Imagine a digital nomad in Buenos Aires. The co-working space internet breaks just before a meeting. The impulse to declare, "Working overseas is hopeless; nothing works here," mounts. Yet, flipping the mental script offers relief. Instead of rigidly interpreting the disruption as incompetence or a hostile environment, practice exploring mental opposites.

## Exercise: "Mental Opposites" for Cognitive Flexibility

- When adversity strikes, pause to identify your first, most negative explanation.

- List two or three additional reasons for the situation that are plausible. For example: The internet failed because of routine maintenance, high regional demand, or simple bad luck.

- Ask how each explanation changes your emotional response. Is there room for problem-solving or empathy?

- Choose the most balanced explanation, and use it as your next action cue: "Maybe this was bad timing, so I'll find a backup spot or inform my team honestly."

By approaching challenges through multiple interpretive lenses, emotional tension softens into workable options.

Building this internal strength further hinges on ritual. Everyday resilience rituals become anchors in the haze of cultural transition. These rituals do not need grandeur—consistency matters more than complexity. A morning affirmation, such as "I face new experiences with curiosity and patience," can create an early psychological buffer. Lighting a scented candle each evening offers a moment of pause and reflection after a day of uncertainty. Each acts as a reminder that stability can arise from repeated, self-chosen actions—even in environments that feel foreign.

## Exercise: Creating a Resilience Ritual

- Select a short phrase or mantra that addresses your current strength or aspiration, such as "Steady in change," or "I adapt, I grow."

- Write it on a sticky note and place it somewhere visible.

- Each morning, recite this phrase while breathing deeply three times.

- Let the ritual mark the transition from preparation to engagement with the day ahead.

Small daily practices lay layers of emotional security that gradually resist the tug of foreignness and fatigue.

Success on the global move often blooms from small victories, not sweeping achievements. Each practical win—navigating the subway for the first time, handling an official document, or ordering food without assistance—feeds persistence. Noticing and celebrating these moments nurtures growth. Rather than waiting for perfection, identifying the progress of "I managed the market by myself" strengthens morale and increases motivation to persevere, even after setbacks.

### Exercise: Celebrating Small Victories

1. Create a "success notebook" in your phone or journal.

2. Each day, jot down one challenge you navigated, no matter how minor.

3. Take a brief moment to savor the feeling of accomplishment—walk around the block, smile in the mirror, or share the anecdote with a friend.

4. Reflect on how each recorded moment signals adaptation and resilience.

Recognition of incremental progress fosters a growth mindset and keeps momentum alive during periods of doubt or exhaustion. Noting these successes grounds resilience, preparing expats for more relentless challenges, both emotional and physical, which often show their first signs through body and energy cues—topics that next demand attention.

## Addressing Stress, Social Withdrawal, and Practicing Mindfulness Abroad

Living far from home, the line between everyday resilience and creeping burnout can blur in subtle ways. For many expats, the earliest warnings often surface not as big breakdowns but as small, almost invisible, shifts in social rhythms. Consider the woman who, after months adjusting to a new city, politely declines her neighbor's rooftop dinner, lets her mother's call go unanswered, and chooses solitude over joining a weekend walk with colleagues. At first, these choices feel like normal self-care, but as days become weeks, the pattern grows. Lunches are always alone, invitations unopened, community events skipped—not because rest is needed, but because connection feels too costly.

Left unattended, these avoidances feed isolation. What begins as recharging soon saps energy, making each new invitation heavier and every missed conversation a tally against motivation. In an environment without family hugs or old friends a short drive away, loneliness can quietly nest in even the busiest routines.

## Spotting the Drift: A Simple Daily Check-In

Tracking these shifts doesn't require an elaborate journal. Jotting down tiny daily notes—like "ate lunch alone 5 days in a row," or "ignored a friend's message" or "avoided a regular call"—can highlight a slide from healthy boundaries into withdrawal. The goal isn't to judge or criticize but to gently witness when distance from others stops being restorative and becomes isolating. This log becomes a mirror, showing patterns that, once named, invite gentle reconnection.

## Knowing When to Seek Help

The adjustment phase in a new country naturally brings stress—language mishaps, cultural misunderstandings, days that feel out of sync. It's normal to feel off for a few days or to crave privacy. Yet, clear markers point to a deeper struggle: persistent trouble concentrating, sadness or irritability lasting more than two weeks, or daily tasks that become steep hills rather than gentle slopes. When these feelings linger, especially without an obvious cause, reaching out for support is an essential act of self-care.

Barriers often stand in the way—maybe the local language is just out of reach, or there's fear of being misunderstood or appearing weak. For many, cultural stigma makes talking about mental health taboo. Practical steps sidestep some of these obstacles: searching for counseling in your home language through remote platforms, posting in expat forums for recommendations, or drafting a brief message to a trusted coworker saying, "Do you know of someone I could talk to?" These conversations are acts of strength—a resourceful, culturally informed way to build new support, not admissions of defeat.

## Anchoring with Mindful Grounding

On difficult days, even a noisy city can offer moments of calm. Mindful grounding, a way to regulate rising emotions, turns noticing the world into an anchor. Find a safe spot—a balcony, a park bench, the corner of a bustling café. For the first minute, let your gaze settle on the details around you: the gentle pattern of bricks, the shifting play of sidewalk shadows, colors of clothing. Next, let your ears explore: maybe the low hum of a fridge, a distant siren, the laughter from a nearby table. Then, shift inward; feel the seat under you, the weight in your palms, the warmth or coolness of air. Repeat this, three minutes at a time, several cycles if needed.

Outside a Seoul metro, a newcomer, overwhelmed by unfamiliar signs and noise, sits at a street café. Instead of escaping inward, she counts the passing umbrellas, notes the pitch of voices, and feels the solidity of the pavement beneath her feet. In this, she finds a momentary sense of home.

## Rituals of Pause

Tiny, portable meditation breaks—Rituals of Pause—can be woven into the busiest schedules. At any moment, pause. Draw three slow, deliberate breaths, releasing tension with each exhale while mentally repeating "release." Let emotions and worries drift like clouds; observe them, resist judging or grasping. These rituals, needing no special skill or technology, offer moments of calm in a noisy world: in elevators, an office bathroom, during a hurried commute.

A basic breathwork routine supports this grounded state: inhale for four counts, hold for four, exhale for four, repeated four times. Use it before meetings, in waiting rooms, after tough conversations—whenever agitation stirs.

## Everyday Expressive Journaling

Layering in one more tool, set aside five minutes at day's end. Write down one emotion felt and one trigger, including cultural specifics like, "Felt frustrated after a miscommunication at the grocery store." Over time, these fragments reveal not just struggle, but progress—the slow victories and persistent pain points, patterns that illuminate both hardship and growth.

These practices flex with each culture and context, offering steadying rituals that transcend borders. Next, the focus will shift from managing difficulty toward building small pockets of joy and gratitude, deepening the roots of well-being in day-to-day expat life.

## Cultivating Joy, Gratitude, and Connection Across Distances

Rain pattered softly against Phuong's apartment window in Berlin, gray light filling her kitchen as she struggled to shake off a restless heaviness. Thousands of kilometers from home, the smallest daily troubles could feel magnified. Yet on her counter sat a worn notebook, filled each night with three short sentences about things that had made her smile or eased her day: the friendly barista who gave her a free pastry, a stranger's compliment in broken German, the sweet memory of her grandmother's soup. Gratitude rituals like Phuong's offer a way to intentionally shift focus, catching flashes of the good—even when loneliness or worry seem loudest. The simple act of seeking and recording positives, especially during rough patches, slowly rewires the mind's habits: small joys become more visible, easier to feel, and gradually, emotional resilience strengthens.

To start a gratitude journal tailored to expat life, follow these steps:

- Pick a specific time every day to reflect on your experiences

- Write down three things that brightened your day abroad—a kind gesture, a new food, a funny mishap, a view that made you pause

- Be specific; instead of "had a good meal," write "tried street corn from the vendor by the metro, tasted smoky and sweet"

- Keep your journal where you'll see it—a bedside table, backpack, or phone app

- When someone is kind or you achieve a small victory, say "thank you" aloud or in your mind

- If language is a barrier, smile, gesture, or write your gratitude in your journal

- Reread old entries on tough days to remind yourself of what's gone right

A burst of drumming and laughter echoed down the street in Porto, drawing Marta, a digital nomad, out from behind her laptop. She peered around the corner and saw her neighborhood transformed for São João Festival—colorful lanterns, locals grilling sardines, families dancing in the streets. Joining community festivities, even as an outsider, cracks open new channels for joy and connection. Local celebrations present opportunities to witness, learn, and participate—igniting a sense of belonging and the dopamine rush of novelty. The act of moving from observer to participant often takes courage but can quickly melt isolation, as even small exchanges—sharing food, learning a folk dance, laughing at your own language mistakes—forge invisible threads of connection.

To engage in local cultural events:

- Research upcoming holidays, market days, or religious festivals in your area; use community boards, WhatsApp groups, or local expat forums

- Choose one event that fits your comfort zone and schedule

- Find out what, if anything, you should bring or wear—ask a neighbor or search event details

- Arrive with openness: your goal is to observe, listen, and learn before joining in

- Step into conversations when possible; use polite greetings and show surprise or delight at unfamiliar rituals

- Offer to help or accept invitations, even if you only stay a short while

- Note the reactions and connections you create, however small, in your gratitude journal that evening

Time can blur while abroad, and personal efforts may slip by unrecognized without the social scaffolding of home. This is where personal milestones—custom holidays or self-made rituals—become powerful antidotes to invisibility. An international student, Tess, realized her one-year anniversary in Barcelona coincided with the day she finally gave directions to a lost tourist in Spanish. Alone in her favorite café, she ordered a celebratory pastry and left herself a congratulatory postcard. These private markers of progress, no matter how playful, dignify growth and break up long stretches of uncertainty or sameness.

To create and honor personal milestones:

- List experiences or dates that feel meaningful, such as your landing date, first local friend, or first job contract abroad

- Pick one upcoming milestone and decide how to mark it—a treat, solo outing, creative project, or video call

- Craft a simple ritual: light a candle, write a letter to yourself, or take a photo in a special place

- If shared moments matter, invite a friend in person or virtually to join your ritual

- Make notes about what the day means to you and how you've grown since arriving

Distance can stretch thin the ties that ground you, but reaching out with joy or thanks generates connection that echoes both ways. Lucas, a Brazilian engineer in Toronto, felt far from family holidays—so he gathered old friends and relatives on a video call for a virtual "Friends-giving," sharing what they missed about home and what they were grateful for in their adopted cities. Their screens lit up with laughter and unexpected stories, many saved in a group gratitude letter that circled their WhatsApp chat for weeks afterward. Intentionally sending gratitude outwards can lift both sender and receiver—reminding you of who cares, and keeping homesickness at bay.

For sharing joy and gratitude with loved ones:

- Choose a special occasion or ordinary day when connections feel thin

- Set a date and time for a virtual gathering or group call; send invitations in advance

- Suggest a theme, such as sharing good news, "something I'm grateful for," or stories from your new place

- For gratitude letters, start a group message or shared document; invite everyone to add a note, memory, or photo

- During the meeting or in your letter, express what you appreciate about each person

- Save the messages or record the call to revisit during lonely times

Moments of joy and gratitude are often cultivated, not stumbled upon. With daily practice—alone and with others—these simple acts become lifelines that weather emotional storms and slowly transform an unfamiliar place into somewhere you can thrive.

## Final Thoughts

Now that we understand how building emotional resilience requires both inward reflection and outward connection, expats can approach life abroad with greater confidence and calm. By recognizing early signs of burnout, challenging negative self-talk, and embracing mindful practices, individuals create a solid foundation for managing stress and uncertainty. Layering in rituals of gratitude and celebrating small victories not only nurtures joy but also strengthens ties to new communities and loved ones far away. With these tools, the journey of adaptation becomes less daunting and more rewarding, empowering expats to thrive emotionally as they navigate the rich complexities of their new lives overseas.

# Love, Family, and Romance Abroad: Reimagined Connections

Have you ever paused to consider how love changes when the familiar turns foreign? What happens to family bonds stretched across time zones and cultures, or to parenting when the rules at home no longer apply? Living abroad reshapes not only where we are but how we connect with those closest to us. It asks us to rethink what it means to belong, to trust, and to care in environments that don't always share our ways of showing affection or support. Navigating these shifts can bring moments of confusion, discomfort, and even heartbreak—but also opportunities for creativity, resilience, and growth. This chapter invites you to reflect on these complex experiences and discover how relationships transform when life takes root beyond borders.

## Intimate Relationships Across Borders: Joys, Challenges, and Healing After Loss

When you fall in love in a new country, everything that once seemed obvious can suddenly feel up for negotiation. An expat might step into a partner's home during a major holiday, eager to experience the warmth of a family gathering, only to realize that what counts as loving involvement varies dramatically. Perhaps dinner comes with blunt questions from relatives—about marriage, children, career plans—delivered with a seriousness that feels foreign and intrusive. For someone from a more private background, these questions might trigger discomfort or even resentment, while their partner interprets them as loving concern.

Misunderstandings can emerge over simple things. One couple, she from Sweden and he from southern Italy, laughed about their first shared Christmas. She planned a quiet evening, but he expected a full-scale family feast, complete with cousins, grandparents, and hours-long debates over food. Her hesitation seemed cold, even distant, to his family. They later joked that "Swedish quiet might be Italian confusion." By talking through what each tradition meant, they discovered a space for both—her calm focus on close connection, his passion for exuberant gatherings. Every year since, they blend the traditions. After a boisterous dinner, they carve out twenty minutes of silence and reflection, honoring her roots without sacrificing his. Blending rituals like this is not a surface compromise but a creative layering of values. In making these "us" traditions, couples build a shared identity strong enough to weather moments of friction.

Language trips can forge intimacy as well as awkwardness. A woman from the United States recalled her relationship with a Japanese partner, where a tiny language slip changed the mood. Meant to tell him, "Your cooking is the best," she accidentally said his food was "definitely weird." Both froze before laughter took over, dissolving tension and deepening trust. Small mistakes—especially those fueled by nerves or unfamiliarity—can become inside jokes. The key was addressing the embarrassment with openness and inviting humor into the moment. When couples acknowledge these moments without shame, intimacy grows. Their shared willingness to stumble and re-cover together, laughing at what might otherwise hurt, forges deeper connection and dismantles fear of getting it wrong.

To prevent misunderstanding and unmet expectations, challenge assumptions early. Partners from different cultures might expect spe-cific signs of commitment; for one, meeting the family means a se-rious intention, while for another, it's casual. Navigating this terrain calls for clarity. State what you expect, listen to what feels serious or light-hearted to your partner, and revisit these expectations over time. When in doubt, ask outright. These candid check-ins can head off bruised feelings and reinforce that each person's perspective is valid, even if unfamiliar.

Everyday routines can also become sites of cross-cultural creativity. One couple developed the ritual of morning coffee—the South Amer-ican partner made strong black coffee, while her French partner baked small croissants. Each brought the tastes of home into a single morn-ing ritual. These tiny daily choices fuse backgrounds: a table holding two cultures, anchored by affection and the intention to meet each other halfway. What makes these rituals powerful is not just novelty but the reassurance of regular, reliable "we-ness." This combined daily habit says, "We choose each other," every morning.

When relationships break down abroad, the challenges deepen. Friends and family often live continents away, unable to comfort in person. Local customs around loss may clash with your own; public grieving could draw sympathy, or be met with confusion. Institutional resources like counseling can feel daunting to access if language or cultural norms differ. In the middle of heartbreak, even simple tasks—grocery shopping or getting out of bed—seem heavier when comfort is distant.

A self-help exercise for emotional recovery begins with reclaiming a sense of independence.

1. Choose the moment in your day that feels the loneliest—perhaps after work or before sleep.

2. Pick one activity you already enjoy, and one completely new to you.

3. Prepare your space so you feel safe and settled: light a candle, make tea, clear clutter.

4. Repeat these activities daily at the same hour, noting which lifts your mood.
   This ritual redefines a formerly painful point in the day and anchors you in possibility rather than loss.

Another method focuses on self-compassion. Self-doubt and blame are common after relationship loss, especially when far from home.

1. Each morning, write a supportive, gentle message to yourself in a journal.

2. In the evening, speak these words aloud.

3. When negative thoughts arise, put them on paper and reply to each as a friend would—offering comfort or realistic reassurance.
   Practicing self-compassion softens self-criticism and, with

repetition, sets a kinder inner tone. Outcomes often include reduced self-blame, a greater sense of steadiness, and
an openness to hope.

During crisis, seeking support matters. One expat reached out to
a community language group and found empathetic listeners who
had faced similar heartbreaks. To find support, check expat forums,
local mental health resources, or cultural organizations. Ask about
English-speaking counselors or group meetings. Taking that first
step—sending a message or going to an event—can shrink isolation.
Remember, as romantic love ebbs or changes, the task of nurturing
distant family bonds remains, often all the more pressing in times
of change. Embracing empathy, humor, and creative routines draws
resilience from each new beginning and loss abroad.

## Family Ties at a Distance: Creative Strategies for Connection

The pull of family does not loosen in the expat experience; if anything, the distance sharpens its edge. For many, rituals become a lifeline—a way to infuse rhythm and intent into relationships strained by
time zones and foreign landscapes. Families who once connected by
sharing breakfast or unwinding together after work must now shape
new habits of togetherness. A family scattered between Tokyo, Berlin,
and São Paulo might schedule a standing Sunday video call, tying
all parties to a shared moment regardless of local time. The clock's
hands point differently in each city, but the call draws everyone into
the same emotional space. These rituals foster anticipation, inviting
a sense of excitement into the fabric of family life: a planned movie
night, watched together on synchronized screens, creates an occasion

to laugh, groan at plot twists, and experience the familiar comfort of shared entertainment.

Virtual meals take on their own kind of intimacy. One family might share recipes ahead of time, prepare the same dishes, and eat while facing each other onscreen. Despite the thousands of miles in between, familiar aromas and family jokes fill the digital space. Special touches give these routines additional meaning—a monthly "time zone toast" where each member raises their glass when the clock strikes 7:00 PM in their country, toasting new jobs, birthdays, or simply the continuation of their shared story. Technology enables holiday traditions to live on in creative form: cousins open gifts together on camera; families light holiday candles, tell stories, and sing songs that echo through speakers across continents. The simple act of marking the calendar with these events creates a sense of belonging, quietly reinforcing the bonds that distance threatens to weaken.

Even outside these regular rituals, digital technology steps in to keep families woven together in daily life. Messaging apps allow for ongoing group chats—short check-ins, inside jokes, support when the day's frustrations tip over. The casual "good morning!" or "look what I made for dinner" sends a ripple of presence through the whole family. Grandparents might read a favorite bedtime book over video, their voice offering reassurance as a child drifts to sleep thousands of miles away. Siblings, grown and living in separate countries, might maintain a playful running commentary on news events, movies, or childhood memories in a shared chat, the flow of conversation picking up and dropping off in a uniquely digital but intimate rhythm.

Collaborative digital journals become archives of shared memory. Families contribute photos, snippets of daily routines, or recordings of laughter and conversation. These living documents grow slowly, accumulating meaning with each entry. On hard days, a parent can flip through and find evidence of their own resilience, or send a favorite photo as a gentle reminder that history and affection endure.

Long-distance family bonds, however, are not maintained without cost. The pangs of guilt and grief frequently surface, often sparked by missed milestones—a wedding unspoken of until photos arrive, a funeral attended only through a blurry livestream, a child's first steps narrated across a shaky internet connection. The ache of absence can feel acute during family emergencies or joyful events, stirring feelings of helplessness and regret. For adult children, the concern over aging parents can grow acute, complicated by a sense of powerlessness that no video call can soothe.

Healthy coping strategies become essential. Families who openly acknowledge their feelings—who say aloud, "I miss you" or "I wish I could be there"—normalize grief and reduce the stigma of sadness. Scheduled times to reflect together, perhaps around significant dates like anniversaries or birthdays, can help families process emotions collectively. Rituals of remembrance, such as lighting a candle or sharing stories on marked days, create opportunities to honor both absence and presence, maintaining an emotional solidarity that distance cannot erase.

Celebrating from afar calls for fresh creativity. Virtual birthday parties may involve coordinated deliveries of cake or decorations, so all members can experience the same sensory delight. A family might organize a surprise exchange, sending small tokens to each other and opening them on camera, recreating the suspense and camaraderie of in-person gatherings. Longstanding customs—like annual holiday recipes or traditional games—find new life as family members establish new rules to suit the digital format. Such adaptations become memories in their own right, blending nostalgia with invention.

These approaches, while rooted in digital solutions, work because they reflect an ongoing willingness to adapt—to carve out meaningful connections, even from within a patchwork of cities and continents. As the chapter continues, the stories of families building these bridges serve as a foundation for understanding the even more intricate realities faced by those raising children abroad, where cross-cultural adaptation adds new layers to the art of sustaining love and belonging.

## Raising Children Abroad: Parenting Strategies for New Norms and Identities

Emotional distance often lingers even within the same household for expatriate parents. While navigating separation from grandparents, siblings, or close friends across countries, parents must create new threads of connection within their own homes. Children can experience this dislocation intensely, especially as the family's daily routines and interactions reflect a blend of unfamiliar customs and lingering nostalgia for what they left behind. When evening settles in and parents attempt to reconnect through bedtime stories, the choice of language and content becomes meaningful. Reading favorite books from home in the heritage language can offer comfort, while picking up stories or television shows from the host country provides context for the new world outside. One parent described their daughter gradually switching from speaking only Spanish at home to mixing in German, the language of their new city. Rather than correcting her, they gently folded both languages into dinnertime conversation, making each one an active tool rather than an obstacle or battleground.

## Supporting Multilingual Development

Raising children to navigate more than one language is both exciting and daunting. Many expat parents hope their children will become truly bilingual, able to speak fluently with relatives back home and participate with ease in their new community. However, this does not happen passively. Consistency makes a difference. Parents who set aside certain times of day for each language, or who alternate which parent speaks which language, find that children quickly learn the value of switching codes. Regular routines, like Sunday video calls with grandparents conducted in the heritage language, reinforce what might otherwise fade into the background. Some families maintain "heritage language hours" where only the home language is spoken, using games, songs, and even kitchen tasks to bring words to life.

There are days when children reject their heritage language, finding it easier or cooler to use the local tongue. In these moments, pressure or frustration can easily damage motivation. Instead, some parents simply model pride and patience, letting the heritage language remain present through music or favorite movies. A family from Turkey living in Norway resorted to watching Turkish cartoons before school, finding this simple ritual enough to keep their son curious about his roots without insisting he use Turkish with his Norwegian friends. Maintaining this flexible, nonjudgmental environment encourages children to see both languages as assets.

## Approaches to Discipline and Autonomy

Discipline styles and expectations may clash powerfully with the customs in a host country. In Japan, for example, group harmony and subtle redirection are often valued, while a German family may expect direct reasoning and clear boundaries. Parents must decide how much to adapt to these norms. One American mother in Singapore observed that her daughter's classmates were allowed much more independence at a younger age—taking public transit alone and spending hours on homework without parents checking. Over time, she eased her own rules, letting her daughter travel with friends, but retained family dinners and rules about screen time.

These adaptations are not betrayals of values but reflections of respect for the new context. An effective approach is explaining to children why differences exist, making household rules transparent and shaped by discussion instead of simple assertion. Teachers, friends, and extended local family become informal guides, offering context when expectations seem unclear. Balancing clarity about family values—such as kindness or fairness—while being open to adjusting other practices can help children see themselves as competent actors in both cultures.

## Deciding on Schools

Educational choices become pivotal for expat families. Enrolling in a local school offers children deep exposure to the language and social fabric of the host culture. Daily routines include local holidays, food at the cafeteria, and friendships that anchor them to their new surroundings. However, local curricula may differ in structure or expectations, challenging students used to other styles. Alternatively, international schools provide continuity, often using familiar curricula, and cultivating communities of other expat children. This can reduce language shock and offer a soft landing, but sometimes at the expense of deep cultural immersion.

One family moving to France found that their eldest thrived in an international school where her British literature studies matched those back home, but her younger brother felt isolated, missing the lively exchanges he saw at the neighborhood French school. For such families, mixing approaches—enlisting tutors, participating in community activities, or shifting schools after a year—can help find the right balance.

## Identity and the Third Culture Kid

Children who spend their formative years outside their parents' home country often emerge as "Third Culture Kids." These young people own pieces of many places, yet may struggle to identify with any one country or group. They can feel rootless, especially if asked, "Where are you from?" at school. Families can ease this tension by validating all parts of their children's identities, encouraging them to share stories about both their origins and new experiences.

Frequent discussions about holidays, family stories, or even cooking traditional meals help children integrate their backgrounds with their everyday life. Some join expat or heritage clubs, others volunteer locally, and many keep journals or art projects exploring what home means to them. Families who nurture this blend without requiring loyalty to just one culture foster children who are flexible, open, and resilient, able to define themselves on their own terms.

## Bringing It All Together

Now that we understand the complex emotions and practical challenges of maintaining love, family bonds, and parenting across cultures and distances, we can embrace these experiences as opportunities for growth and connection. By openly communicating expectations, creating new shared rituals, and practicing patience with ourselves and our children, expats can build resilient relationships that honor both their roots and their current lives. Although distance may bring moments of loneliness and cultural confusion, it also invites creativity and empathy, helping us forge unique identities and communities that transcend borders. With this awareness and these tools, those living abroad can move forward with greater confidence, knowing that love and family—though transformed—remain at the heart of a fulfilling expat journey.

# Great Expectations: Managing Hopes and Realities

Living abroad often begins with high hopes fueled by stories of adventure, success, and personal transformation. Yet the reality frequently presents a mix of excitement and unexpected challenges that test resilience and adaptability. Many newcomers find themselves navigating not only new cultures and languages but also myths and assumptions about what expat life should be like. These misconceptions can create frustration when actual experiences fall short of idealized expectations.

This chapter examines how to bridge the gap between hopes and realities in the expatriate journey. It offers insights into recognizing common myths, setting practical expectations, managing setbacks, and adjusting personal goals with flexibility. By exploring strategies for resilience and emotional growth, readers will gain tools to foster deeper satisfaction and success while living abroad.

## Myth-Busting and Setting Practical Expectations

Shiny photos on social media often show expatriate life as an endless parade of beautiful cafes, breathtaking beaches, and sunlit adventures. Scroll through any feed, and you may see new arrivals grinning with gelato in hand or laughing in front of famous landmarks. These carefully posed, filtered images give the impression that life abroad means instant happiness and effortless success. Yet, what's left out of these posts tells a different story. Consider the story of Sarah, who moved to Rome and filled her feed with pictures of cobblestone streets and aperitivo hour, never mentioning the struggle she faced trying to set up a bank account with limited Italian or the hours spent lost on public transport. Another expat, Rahul, posted daily views from his Paris apartment, but online he hid the evenings he spent alone, missing family and battling homesickness.

People consuming these images often begin to internalize a sense of inadequacy when their own experience doesn't match the highlight reel. The contrast between curated, celebratory snapshots and the reality of daily frustrations can spark self-doubt and shame. It's easy to believe you're the only one facing bureaucratic tangles, language slips, or unwelcoming stares. Social media rarely captures the phone calls to embassies that stretch into weeks, the endless paperwork for residency permits, or the tension of trying to make a new friend in an unfamiliar language. These "Instagram illusions" can become powerful myths, fueling the false expectation that adaptation should be easy and seamless.

Another myth that shapes expectations is the idea that living abroad is the same as being on vacation. While new places feel exciting at first, daily life quickly emerges with its own set of routines, obligations, and complexities. Imagine the first few weeks in a new country when the initial thrill fades and the search for a job becomes urgent. The story of Julia, who arrived in Barcelona and spent the first month exploring, illustrates this shift. She soon ran up against the slow process of navigating unfamiliar job markets, dealing with paperwork in Spanish, and coping with dwindling savings. Evenings once filled with tapas crawls transitioned to stress over paying rent.

Settling abroad also means dealing with mundane frustrations. Grocery shopping might turn into a puzzle when labels are undecipherable. A doctor's appointment could be stressful if nobody speaks your language. Such daily realities often bring emotional fatigue. The challenge goes beyond paperwork. When friendships at home feel distant and building new social ties takes longer than hoped, it is normal to feel isolated or disoriented. Recognizing struggle as a real part of the process—rather than proof of personal failure—helps people avoid unhealthy comparison with online images or the myth of effortless adventure.

Work-life balance often changes shape in a new country. Many move abroad for professional reasons, seeking advancement or a fresh start, only to discover that career paths rarely transfer directly across borders. An engineer from the U.S. may find professional norms entirely different in Germany and discover that networking requires new skills. Others, like Sam who moved to Thailand, realize that steady jobs pay less or require local qualifications. Sam embraced freelance work, which offered flexibility and creative freedom, but also accepted that rapid progress up the career ladder would slow. In another example, Maya discovered that status and titles mattered less in her new

community in Portugal than contributing to local causes. She shifted her focus to volunteering and found personal fulfillment separate
from her former job title. This recalibration is common. Sometimes it
means redefining success by quality of life or community, rather than
traditional career milestones.

Perspective and privilege play a significant role in how expat life
unfolds. Those who speak the local language or have strong savings
account benefit from smoother transitions. For instance, Tom, whose
company handled every logistical step, found it easier to adapt than
Ana, who arrived alone and had to confront every obstacle herself.
Visa limitations, income requirements, and experiences of prejudice
form real hurdles for many. Lia, a student from Brazil in Germany,
dealt with relentless paperwork and stereotyping. Meanwhile, Lin
from Singapore found that financial security allowed for more frequent travel home and the option to seek paid help with tasks.

Recognizing your own position in this landscape provides valuable
perspective. Honesty about what makes your journey easier or harder
builds empathy for other expats with different backgrounds. It also
clarifies what realistic goals and strategies for support may look like.

Hoping for unbroken happiness abroad can lead to disappointment when reality intrudes. Instead, preparing for setbacks offers real
advantages. Learning basic phrases, budgeting for unexpected expenses, and choosing neighborly neighborhoods set the stage for resilience.
Practicing patience with yourself and others lessens the shock when
things go wrong. As you anticipate difficulties and rehearse possible
responses, you grow more confident facing obstacles and more flexible
in adapting goals. This mindset favors growth over perfection, setting
up the foundation for a more rewarding and balanced expat experience.

## Resilience Strategies and Growth Through Disappointments

For many moving abroad, the moment when daily life starts to clash with cherished expectations can feel jarring. That initial vision—perhaps an effortless social circle or seamless career advancement—suddenly faces realities like cultural nuances, bureaucratic hurdles, or moments of loneliness that no amount of prior research could have fully anticipated. Far from being signs of failure or defeat, these experiences mark the beginning of an essential emotional journey. Making space for setbacks transforms them from burdens into building blocks.

Adjusting to a new country often means normalizing the idea that mistakes and awkward missteps are not just probable, but necessary. Consider the expat who misinterprets a local custom at a community gathering, accidentally offending their host by arriving late, believing it fashionable when in fact it is rude in that context. Or the new hire who fumbles through a business meeting, discovering mid-presentation that the casual style embraced back home is read as unprofessional in the new workplace. These moments can sting, but by seeing them as expected chapters in the adaptation process, their emotional weight softens. The fear of making mistakes lessens with each minor failure that passes without lasting consequence. Over time, the realization grows that perfectionism is not the goal—adaptability is.

### From Stumbles to Self-Awareness

Clear-eyed examination of setbacks can spark self-awareness that would have been difficult to access in more familiar surroundings. A miscommunication with a landlord or a critical performance review may be uncomfortable, but reviewing these incidents allows expats to spot cultural assumptions or emotional triggers previously hidden from their view. By naming the frustration or embarrassment, asking what went wrong, and considering how different behavior would have changed the outcome, expats can begin to replace defensiveness with curiosity.

This process—sometimes called emotional alchemy—transforms disappointment into momentum for change. Imagine an expat who faces professional rejection after applying for a coveted job. At first, discouragement might hover for days. Instead of dismissing the emotion or escaping into distractions, sitting with the disappointment can reveal its components: perhaps specific skills to work on, gaps in language proficiency, or even personal ideals in need of adjustment. With these insights in hand, motivation grows to enroll in new classes, seek honest feedback, or pursue alternative roles that align more closely with strengths. What began as a setback evolves into purposeful action, fueled by the desire to navigate future challenges with greater skill.

## Emphasizing the Value of Resilience

While initial victories in a new country are celebrated, it is in the recovery from setbacks that lasting growth emerges. Recovery, rather than unbroken success, deserves recognition. A serial miscommunicator at first, the resilient expat learns to laugh at minor blunders and tries again, each time with more skill. An anecdote often shared describes someone who spent their early months never quite understanding neighborhood etiquette. Repeated awkward moments, like inadvertently skipping queues or misreading invitations, gave way to asking questions, observing others, and gradually mastering the local flow. Over time, their confidence returned, not because mistakes stopped happening, but because each recovery brought resourcefulness and humility. This kind of bounce-back experience helps to forge a durable sense of self-worth, distinct from fleeting first wins.

## Expanding Strategies Through Local Wisdom

Expatriate adjustment broadens when newcomers draw on local knowledge and community practices for handling setbacks. Watching how neighbors, co-workers, or acquaintances recover and adapt can illuminate options expats may not have considered. For instance, some societies approach setbacks not with silent embarrassment, but with open communal support. The local tradition of gathering after a difficult week, sharing stories and laughter, may provide an approach to disappointments that replaces solitary rumination with shared resilience.

A casual invitation to participate in a neighborhood project or local festival can open doors to subtle insights—maybe witnessing a friend patiently repairing a problem rather than abandoning it, or listening as a neighbor recounts their own early misadventures adjusting to the same city. Adopting these community-based responses invites greater empathy, patience, and versatility into an expat's toolkit. Over time, these borrowed strategies blend with personal coping styles, empowering expats to respond to adversity with new confidence and understanding.

Gradually, as the emotional terrain grows more familiar, expats may notice their old definitions of success and fulfillment start to shift. Early disappointments, once dreaded, become guides that point toward previously unimagined motivations and evolving priorities. This unfolding path encourages a flexible approach to long-term aims, inviting continual adaptation and renewed energy—qualities essential for meaningful life abroad.

## Realigning Goals and Motivations: Flexible Self-Help Exercises

Moving through another unfamiliar city, an international student notices the ways her dreams shift with each season. At first, she planned to master the local language within a year, imagining academic accolades and expert-level conversation. Only months later, finding herself isolated, she feels her priorities leaning elsewhere. Loneliness brings a new urgency, and she sees that friendship matters more than flawless grammar. This is an ordinary expat pattern: ambitions change shape as daily life teaches what is truly needed.

### Goal Shuffling

This exercise starts with a written list of your current goals. Look them over and ask which ones truly fit your day-to-day reality now. For each, consider if it connects to your core values or has become a leftover expectation. Place a checkmark next to goals that still feel right; strike through those that no longer fit; highlight any that feel unfamiliar or imposed. Choose one or two less relevant aims and consciously push them aside. Focus your attention on a smaller set that resonates deeply with the present.

A student in Madrid, Pablo, aimed to become fluent in Spanish swiftly. But after late-night conversations in broken phrases and shared laughter, he recognizes friendship is more rewarding than linguistic perfection. He moves "make local friends" to the top of his goal list, reducing pressure on rapid language mastery. With this shift, each day feels lighter and more meaningful.

Practicing Goal Shuffling encourages regular realignment. It turns overwhelming lists into sets of living ambitions, allowing for the discarding of old goals without guilt. By focusing on what matters now, energy is shifted away from outdated objectives and towards pursuits that foster happiness and resilience.

## Motivation Inventory

This method centers on tuning into what brings energy and interest, rather than what "should" inspire you. At the end of each day, set aside ten quiet minutes. Recall specific moments: a task finished, a meal enjoyed, a conversation had. Note your emotions in response—curiosity, frustration, boredom, or delight. Scan for any surge or drop in enthusiasm. Identify any themes that appear more than once over a week: a helpful pattern may emerge.

Consider Nina, a remote worker living in Bali. Despite delivering projects well, she finds herself dreading Monday mornings. Through brief nightly check-ins, she notices her mood brightens whenever she builds something new—a digital prototype, a painted mural, even a revised recipe. She realizes routine task completion drains her, while creative challenges energize her. This realization nudges Nina to propose more inventive projects to her manager and to volunteer for a local community arts event.

Daily Motivation Inventory replaces vague dissatisfaction with clear signals. By giving attention to what truly moves you, it enables decisions rooted in awareness, replacing routine with more intentional living.

## Building a Flexible Life Map

Rather than relying on a single expectation, this approach opens doors to many possible futures. Begin by picturing three versions of yourself: one following your current path, one exploring a tempting alternative, and one taking a surprising direction you have not yet tried. Jot down short scenarios for each version, including new roles, relationships, and routines. Identify one action, however small, that could move you toward each possible outcome in the next week.

Anna, a mid-career expat in Singapore, faces a crossroads. She wonders: Should she stay in her consulting job, join a local nonprofit, or seek fully remote freelance work? She sketches each scenario on paper, listing opportunities and anxieties for each. In one future, she visualizes herself leading a multicultural team; in another, she mentors local youth; and in a third, she embraces global travel with her partner. Anna decides to set up one informational interview in each field, unlocking new possibilities while reducing fear of making the "wrong" choice.

Life Mapping helps break the illusion of permanence and welcomes the idea that life may unfold along several worthy paths. The map becomes more than a plan—it's a tool for embracing uncertainty with curiosity instead of apprehension.

## Letting Go of Stagnation

This exercise targets ambitions that have become sources of frustration or guilt. Begin by listing goals that feel heavy, repetitive, or imposed by past circumstances. Name the emotions attached to each—disappointment, stubbornness, or anxiety. Ask whether you're holding onto an idea because it still brings energy or simply because you always have. Decide to formally release one outdated goal, perhaps writing it down and then throwing away the note, or sharing your new direction with a friend.

Marcus, hoping to launch a coffee shop in Prague, clings to this goal even as costs soar and his health suffers. One afternoon, he admits his motivation now lies elsewhere—he enjoys organizing local park clean-ups, which bring immediate satisfaction and new friends. Letting go of his business plan, he plunges into community life. Marked by this choice, he finds new purpose with less stress.

By letting go of stagnant ambitions, space is created for motivations that reflect who you've become—not just who you once planned to be. These changes invite vitality and authentic self-authorship, essential qualities in building a satisfying, ever-evolving expat experience.

## Bringing It All Together

Now that we understand how myths and unrealistic expectations can cloud the expat experience, we are better equipped to approach life abroad with honesty and flexibility. By acknowledging challenges as natural parts of adaptation and embracing setbacks as opportunities for growth, expats can develop resilience and deepen self-awareness. Adjusting goals and motivations in response to changing realities helps create a more authentic and fulfilling journey. With these perspectives and tools, those living overseas can navigate cultural transitions more confidently, turning disruption into personal growth and building a meaningful life beyond the highlight reel.

# Thriving, Not Surviving: Mastering the Expat Mindset

What does it really take to move beyond simply getting by in a new country and start thriving as an expat? How do you shift your mindset when everything feels unfamiliar, and the pressure to adapt weighs heavily on your shoulders? Is it possible to find a sense of belonging without losing yourself, to embrace cultural differences while staying true to who you are? These questions reveal the heart of what many face when living abroad—not just practical challenges but deep emotional shifts. This chapter explores how cultivating resilience through self-acceptance, flexibility, openness, and thoughtful planning can transform the expat experience from one of survival into one of growth and fulfillment.

## Building Self-Compassion and Adaptability in Unfamiliar Environments

A chill dawn filters through apartment windows in a city that still feels like it belongs to someone else. Karina, an expat a few months into her new life, scrolls through feeds packed with cheerful snapshots from local friends—weekend hikes, language jokes, insider haunts she wouldn't know to find. A knot forms, tight with the thought, "I'm so far behind. I'll never belong here the way they do." This sticky self-judgment is common, especially under the spotlight of cultures that prize adaptation. Radical self-acceptance begins with the understanding that these thoughts are normal—and that interrupting these loops is a daily act of courage.

## Silencing the Comparison Trap: The Mirror Exercise

**Why this works:** Negative self-talk grows in the space between where we think we should be and where we are. By consciously halting those comparisons and tuning into our own story, self-awareness replaces self-criticism.

### How to practice:

1. **Pause when you notice comparison.** Karina, noticing a pang as she scrolls, tells herself to set her phone down.

2. **Label the feeling out loud or in writing.** She says, "I feel less accomplished when I see their posts."

3. **Acknowledge the uniqueness of your path.** She lists recent achievements (navigating public transit, ordering dinner in stumbling but sincere local language, celebrating a small holiday alone).

4. **Ground with sensory mindfulness.** She notices the softness of the morning light, the warmth of her coffee, the hum outside.

5. **Reflect on growth.** Karina says, "I am learning in ways I couldn't have at home."

6. **Repeat as needed, especially after moments that spark insecurity.**

Showing yourself where you are growing—however quietly—replaces hollow comparison with self-anchored respect. Each day, this exercise chips away at the sense of inadequacy, building a pattern of mindful self-awareness equipped to face new challenges.

## Affirmations for Belonging: The Ritual Reminder

**Why this works:** Frequent moments of not-fitting-in can chip away at self-worth. Intentionally repeating a culturally sensitive affirmation grounds confidence and softens alienation by giving the mind a different narrative to follow.

**How to practice:**

1. **Identify a recurring task (making coffee, tying shoes, waiting at a bus stop).**

2. **Craft an affirmation that recognizes your efforts.** For example: "I am carving out my place here, one brave step at a time." For extra potency, use one detail from your host country—a local idiom, a landmark, or even a food—woven in.

3. **Repeat the affirmation each time you perform the cho-**

**sen task.** As Karina stirs her tea each morning, she quietly says her phrase, blending words with action.

4. **Visualize yourself growing roots as you say it, picturing specific ways you have adapted or contributed.**

5. **Acknowledge any resistance or doubt and say the words anyway, allowing them to settle in.**

Over weeks, this affirmation ties a daily habit to self-acceptance, transforming fleeting routines into acts of self-affirmation. The ritual grows into a source of comfort and belonging, especially during moments spent alone.

## Normalizing Vulnerability: Connection Through Openness

**Why this works:** Feeling isolated can fester when struggles remain unspoken. Sharing an honest piece of your experience allows empathy in, transforming loneliness into a channel for connection.

**How to practice—Open Conversation Steps:**

1. **Choose one person you trust—perhaps a fellow expat, mentor, or a local willing to listen.**

2. **Identify one specific struggle (a language error, a cultural miss, a day that felt too heavy).**

3. **Reach out via a short text, message, or in person. For example: "I've had a rough afternoon and could use someone to talk to—do you have a moment?"**

4. **Share your story as plainly as possible, focusing on your**

feelings instead of pretending everything is fine.

5. **Listen to their response and allow yourself to feel seen, even if only for a moment.**

A morning when Karina mispronounced a key phrase, drawing confused stares at a bakery, left her rattled. Sharing this story in a WhatsApp group led to laughter and stories from others, dissolving shame and building real solidarity. Initiating one open conversation normalizes vulnerability as an act of strength, not weakness.

## Rewarding Self-Progress: Milestone Journaling

**Why this works:** Growth often hides in daily friction, escaping notice until doubt creeps in. Collecting milestones and rewarding effort ensures that self-acceptance becomes habit, not exception.

**How to practice:**

1. **Keep a small notebook or app handy.**

2. **At the end of every week, list three wins—large or small. Passing a language exam, introducing yourself to a neighbor, cooking a new dish.**

3. **Set a short-term goal for the next week, such as attending a gathering or reading a local newspaper article.**

4. **Pick a meaningful reward: a favorite treat, a film from home, a stroll in a park. Schedule it in.**

5. **Review progress at month's end, planning new goals and reflecting on personal growth, not comparison.**

Each record becomes proof that thriving is already underway. This concrete record of small successes keeps self-respect growing, anchoring the mindset needed for further adaptation.

Radical self-acceptance, rooted in these practices, gives a sturdy base from which to explore adaptability and open-mindedness. As the journey unfolds, these next approaches will layer on practical skills for ongoing adaptation, drawing power from the deep well of self-compassion first nurtured here.

## Embracing Cultural Differences and Personal Growth Through Open-Minded Engagement

Open-mindedness means more than accepting cultural differences from a distance. For expats, it becomes an essential tool for discovery. Welcoming the unknown changes both the experience and the individual. Curiosity forms the core of open-mindedness. When an expat avoids snap judgments, a pathway opens—not just for understanding etiquette, but also for connecting with the soul of a new place.

One afternoon, a newcomer in a bustling Tokyo district witnesses commuters lining up silently, respecting an unspoken public order. Instead of viewing this restraint as cold or unfriendly, the expat asks herself why personal space might matter more in this setting. She joins the line, chats quietly with someone beside her, and learns that this patience reflects not detachment, but a shared value of harmony. Her search for understanding, not superiority, uncovers something deeper than a list of travel do's and don'ts. In this act of gentle inquiry, she moves past difference as a barrier. This habit, repeated in countless small interactions, gradually replaces the old reflex of labeling what seems unusual as 'incomprehensible.' The shift proves subtle but powerful.

Genuinely seeking out local perspectives transforms interactions. At a Moroccan dinner, a guest notices the host eats using only their right hand. Instead of laughing or feeling annoyed when corrected for doing otherwise, the expat asks about the custom, eager to learn, not just to fit in but to grasp the 'why' behind the action. The conversation reveals layers of history and symbolism. This attitude creates room for the local host to become a guide, not an obstacle. Rather than staying in a cycle of transactional exchanges—'How do I do this?'—the expat's curiosity allows both people to connect on a more meaningful level.

Encountering unfamiliar social cues or traditions sometimes leads to mistakes. Early missteps are nearly inevitable. An expat in Chile, invited to a barbecue, uses "tú" instead of the more formal "usted" with an elder, causing mild embarrassment. Rather than stewing in shame or defensiveness, the expat reflects later, questions friends, and listens carefully at the next gathering. He becomes more attuned to context and relationships. Every blunder shapes awareness, resilience, and skill. Mistakes transform from moments of discomfort into catalyst events for improvement.

The fear of failure can often make expats cautious. However, moments that feel like errors serve as rich teaching laboratories. The key is viewing them with honest curiosity and a willingness to adapt. Asking "What can I take from this?" instead of "Why did I fail?" helps develop both nuance and genuine connection within the host community. These lessons do not solely benefit interactions abroad—they teach a kind of flexibility that travels everywhere.

Returning home after living abroad introduces its own surprises. Many expect comfort and belonging to return automatically, but home changes, too. Often, an expat visits a favorite local café only to feel like an outsider in a place once deeply familiar. The language and rituals come easily, but expectations and worldviews have subtly shifted. Frustration and confusion bubble up. Here, the same open-mindedness used abroad becomes vital. By observing home with fresh eyes and suspending judgment, one can see both personal growth and changes in the community. Reflecting on these shifts, the expat discovers possibilities for meaningful reintegration: joining new circles, sharing international perspectives, or starting a project inspired by lessons learned overseas.

Expanding comfort zones happens in gradual steps, not giant leaps. The most lasting growth occurs during small, intentional experiments: joining a neighborhood festival instead of staying home, signing up for a new class taught in the host language, or striking up a conversation in the local market. At first, anxiety and awkwardness inevitably follow. Inch by inch, these forays make the unfamiliar less daunting. For example, a woman living in Germany signs up for a local pottery workshop. She struggles and makes mistakes, sometimes feeling clumsy, but she eventually forms connections over shared creative challenges. With each session, her sense of belonging and adventure grows stronger.

Pushing the boundaries of comfort—purposely and with care—develops adaptability and a robust sense of self. Noticing discomfort, instead of shying away, reveals the edge of one's current growth. Turning toward those edges, again and again, strengthens resilience and deepens the expat's capacity to thrive. These experiences cultivate a broad perspective and hint at a future shaped by proactive choices, where adaptability and open vision play a central role in lasting fulfillment.

## Visualizing and Creating Sustainable Expat Success Through Long-Term Planning

Stepping into a future as an expat, the difference between just getting by and truly thriving starts with the bold act of shaping one's days instead of letting them just happen. This means trading the scramble to survive for the slow building of a life with intention. The mindset of cultivation translates directly into certain practical habits—planned, revisited, and lived out with heart and flexibility.

### Visioning: Continuously Shaping the Life You Want

Everything begins with visioning—a practice that keeps one's direction clear, even when the road curves.

- **Purpose:** Visioning helps anticipate change, energize goals, and adjust along the way, supporting ongoing self-acceptance and adaptation.

- **Steps:**

1. Set aside time, even just monthly, to imagine your ideal life in your host country. Not just big dreams—get specific about routines, people, and feelings.

2. Write these visions down, sketch them, or create vision boards—any tangible blueprint works.

3. Compare your current reality to this vision: What's aligned, and what isn't?

4. Revise your vision as your needs or circumstances evolve.

5. Set one meaningful, achievable aim based on these revisions.

Sitting at her tiny balcony table, Léa quietly sketches out her third version of a "perfect day abroad" since moving to Vienna. At first, her vision centered on finding cafés like back home—now, it's about balancing university work with bike rides to the river and mastering enough German to join conversations at her art class. Each vision update, done with honesty and kindness toward herself, pulls her closer to a life that grows with her.

## Financial Security: Preparing for the Unseen

Even the most vibrant vision falls apart without practical resources. Financial security is about being future-ready, not just frugal; having a plan means fewer emergencies turn into catastrophes.

- **Purpose:** Preparation for sudden expenses, evolving goals, and fluctuating currencies gives expats peace of mind and agency.

- **Steps:**

1. List all current income, regular expenses, and probable one-off costs—such as visa renewals, flights home, or healthcare.

2. Research local costs and expected fluctuations. Use savings calculators or budgeting apps in your host currency.

3. Build a small cushion for surprises: a new tax, a currency dip, a broken phone.

4. Track expenses weekly at the start, then monthly as habits

settle.

5. Adjust your plan whenever life throws something new—prioritize flexibility over perfection.

When Surya, a newly arrived software engineer, faced a sudden jump in rent after municipal taxes increased, his carefully built "emergency buffer" made the difference. He'd allowed for exactly this sort of swing, so instead of feeling cornered, he adjusted grocery spending for the month, cut a subscription, and connected with friends for a group meal instead of solo dining out. The result was more than financial; security translated to confidence in navigating instability.

## Career Planning: Growing Skills and Opportunity

A thriving career abroad means more than a job—it's participating in a new ecosystem. Adaptability and open-mindedness allow expats to find purpose where they might not have expected.

- **Purpose:** Intentional career planning opens doors, reveals transferable skills, and connects individuals to a sense of belonging in their new environment.

- **Steps:**

1. Research all credential, language, or legal requirements for your profession in the new country.

2. List skills from your home country and brainstorm how they apply locally, even in new sectors.

3. Reach out to local professionals—find meetups, online forums, or expat networking events.

4. Identify one mentor, formal or informal, to ask questions and gain guidance.

5. Evaluate progress every few months and pivot if needed.

Carlos once taught science in Argentina but arrived in Warsaw uncertain of local regulations. He spent evenings joining English-language teacher groups, comparing his certifications and learning that bilingual instruction was in demand at international schools. His new mentor, a fellow expat, guided him past early pitfalls, and when an offer came to design bilingual STEM workshops, he recognized his background was a bridge, not a barrier.

## Endgame Mapping: Choosing What Lasts

The journey of thriving involves knowing not just how to start, but when and whether to end. Planning for the "endgame" is not defeatist—it's self-respecting and adaptable.

- **Purpose:** Endgame planning lets expats choose deliberately—to stay, move on, or return—based on personal growth and set criteria rather than outside pressures.

- **Steps:**

1. Quietly reflect on what fulfillment means to you: connection, security, career, or adventure.

2. Set up a few signals that show whether your needs are still being met—like ongoing enthusiasm, close friendships, or career progress.

3. Every six months, take an honest inventory: Are your criteria

being fulfilled?

4. If not, open the conversation: Is it time to reshape your experience, look for new opportunities, or consider change?

5. Accept your answer with self-compassion, knowing growth sometimes means moving on.

Grace, after five years in Osaka, felt the initial spark fading. She listed what had changed—more tiredness, less exploration, calls home tinged with longing. Reviewing her own markers for satisfaction, she gently asked whether it was time to try somewhere new. With a deep breath, she decided to plan for a year's end move—a choice that felt like honoring herself, not giving up. Self-awareness and open-minded adaptation, learned from her years abroad, allowed her to shape her next adventure as much as the last.

With these future-facing tools, expat life becomes something sculpted, not just endured. Strategic visioning, smart finances, career shaping, and honest self-checks form a loop—each supporting the others, all rooted in an adaptable and self-accepting mindset. The unpredictable world beyond home becomes the creative soil for growth, not a set of obstacles to survive.

## Bringing It All Together

Now that we understand the importance of radical self-acceptance, open-minded engagement, and thoughtful long-term planning, expats can move beyond mere survival to truly thrive in their new environments. Embracing vulnerability and celebrating small wins build a resilient foundation, while curiosity and adaptability open doors to meaningful connections and personal growth. By envisioning the life they want and preparing practically for the future, expats gain confidence and agency over their journey. With these tools, the challenges of cultural transition become opportunities to cultivate strength, belonging, and a flourishing mindset that carries forward whatever path lies ahead.

# Adventures Large and Small: Finding Extraordinary in Everyday

Have you ever noticed how moments that seem small or ordinary can suddenly feel like adventures when you're living in a new place? How does one find excitement beyond the obvious tourist spots or planned activities, uncovering stories hidden in everyday routines? For those who have moved abroad or are preparing to do so, questions often arise about how to stay curious and open when every day brings both the familiar and the unfamiliar. How can simple choices—like taking a different route home or trying an unfamiliar snack—become meaningful parts of a larger journey? This chapter explores ways to recognize and embrace these experiences, helping you turn daily life into a path for personal growth and connection as you navigate the challenges and surprises of living abroad.

## Everyday and Travel Adventures: Finding Growth in the Ordinary and the Journey

A city's daily rhythm, at first glance, can seem predictable. Yet, within familiar routines, powerful adventures hide in plain sight. The idea of micro-adventures finds meaning here: adventure shrinks from epic expeditions to the scale of everyday life, waiting in trips to a corner bakery or evening walks through new backstreets. What transforms these activities from chores into experiences worth retelling is a shift in perspective. The focus moves from efficiency to curiosity, from avoidance of the unfamiliar to intentional exploration.

Exploring a neighborhood on foot reveals small worlds within a city. An expat in Berlin, for example, may start with the practical errand of finding the closest grocery store. Yet, by intentionally choosing an unfamiliar route or a local market in a quieter district, the experience changes. Noticing architectural details—an ornate doorframe, forgotten graffiti, a courtyard garden—each walk uncovers something new. Assigning a playful challenge, such as learning the name of a street passed every day or scanning menus for a dish never tried before, adds structure to discovery. These habits create a sense of progress and transform repetition into growth. The ordinary becomes a series of personal milestones, each one a miniature story layered into the larger narrative of life abroad.

## Ordinary Activities as Gateways to Curiosity

Routine acts, when approached with intention, become invitations to engage. The daily commute holds potential; riding the same bus does not always mean seeing the same city. One day, paying closer attention to fellow passengers' conversations might reveal a popular event or unfamiliar slang. Another, watching the shifting scenery beyond the window sparks interest in a mural or shop that calls for a later detour. Setting a goal to try a new snack at the station stand replaces predictability with anticipation, creating sensory memories attached to place and time.

Meals, traditionally social and sensory, are especially rich territory for micro-adventures. A digital nomad in Hanoi, unsure about a dish, may ask a stall owner for something "local," turning a meal into a lesson in both language and culinary culture. Even a small risk, like sampling an ingredient never encountered before, expands comfort zones. Careful note-taking—recording impressions, learning the names of spices, or snapping a quick photograph—cements these moments as tangible memories.

## Small Social Risks and Language Play

Adventures abroad aren't restricted to the physical world; language is its own terrain. Facing daily conversational challenges, such as greeting a shopkeeper with a newly learned phrase, transforms nervousness into empowerment. Mistakes often create stories of their own, like confusing two similar words or mispronouncing a local name. These errors, rather than sources of embarrassment, become badges of effort and humor. Each exchange builds both skill and confidence. An adult student in Madrid, laughing about calling for "oil" instead of "help" in a market, might later recount that story as proof of progress and adaptability. Over time, such moments accumulate, forging a sense of connection that reaches beyond linguistic accuracy.

Curiosity can be structured into habits. Making it routine to ask a neighbor about the history of a building adds context to surroundings. Observing a plant or a street animal not found at home and recording the discovery with a brief journal entry turns fleeting impressions into a catalog of adaptation. These notes, simple or elaborate, do more than preserve facts: they mark a journey of becoming present within a new culture.

## Storytelling: Discovering Meaning in the Unplanned

Daily experiences, once documented, transform into portable adventures. Writing a brief summary of a day, whether in a notebook or through photos, helps reveal patterns and deeper themes. Comparing organized activities—like a guided city tour—with spontaneous moments, such as a missed train leading to an unexpected street festival, demonstrates the lessons within unpredictability. Structured plans encourage goal setting; meanwhile, mishaps teach emotional agility. A canceled class might allow for a conversation with a stranger over coffee, opening the door to fresh insight or friendship.

Travel stories, even the smallest, become tools for resilience. Sharing an awkward misunderstanding or a sudden change of plans invites laughter and allows for a reframing of difficulties as learning opportunities. Over time, this mindset breeds flexibility and gratitude, skills that make unfamiliar places feel more like home.

Encounters with strangers, often brief but meaningful, remind travelers of the power of presence. Accepting a neighbor's invitation to a local celebration, even awkwardly, may spark memories of connection and cultural insight. Collecting and reflecting on these instances, one builds an inner narrative that steadily expands, transforming ordinary life into a source of adventure, wisdom, and ongoing self-discovery. Each note, photo, or retold story prepares the way for new, unexpected delights along the journey.

## Embracing Serendipity: Making the Most of Unexpected Opportunities

Curiosity and openness form the invisible roots of serendipity in life abroad. The willingness to step beyond what's familiar unlocks interactions and experiences that would never have emerged back home. Adjusting to a new routine in an unfamiliar place sharpens an awareness of small changes and moments that can lead to surprising discoveries. Practicing mindful presence—looking up from a phone, asking questions, or showing genuine interest in surroundings—serves as an invitation for happy accidents. Over time, these habits create an underlying attitude of receptivity, setting the stage for transformation sparked by the unplanned.

### Chance Encounters

Unscripted meetings often bring about the most compelling stories. Casual conversations at neighborhood gatherings, rides on shared transportation, or a friendly exchange at a market can unexpectedly morph into avenues for friendship or collaboration. Take the experience of an American teacher who, while searching for a bookstore in Prague, shared a tram seat with a local artist. Their brief conversation led to an invitation to a gallery opening, eventually blossoming into a creative partnership that lasted years and opened doors in the art community. In another story, a relocating engineer in Argentina attended a language exchange night out of pure curiosity and ended up meeting both a future roommate and a trusted mentor. These aren't just chance meetings—they are catalysts, forged because someone was open, attentive, and eager to connect. Following up on initial sparks—grabbing coffee, sending a thank-you message—turns fleeting contact into life-shaping relationships.

## Accidental Skill Acquisition

Living overseas often means figuring things out that would have fallen to someone else before. Hands-on learning, born from everyday needs or sudden challenges, becomes the norm. Imagine a digital nomad in Lisbon who struggled with apartment repairs and, with the help of a neighbor, learned how to plaster a wall and fix electrical outlets. Instead of frustration, the process became a source of pride and a much-talked-about story at social gatherings. Another scenario: a Canadian student in Japan who joined neighbors in pickling vegetables for a local festival, learning not just recipes but language and cultural nuances. What begins as necessity or curiosity becomes enrichment. These skills are rarely on the checklist before arrival, yet they add depth, adaptability, and a feeling of independence. By viewing the unexpected as a chance to expand, rather than an inconvenience, expats turn their everyday mishaps into building blocks for personal growth.

## Job Offers Out of Nowhere

Professional paths rarely follow a straight line when living away from home. Remaining open and engaged creates fertile ground for opportunities to emerge without warning. Consider a software developer living in Berlin who volunteered at a city hackathon one weekend and, by sharing a few ideas, caught the attention of a small startup urgently seeking a technical lead. The job offer came not from a formal application, but from a spontaneous display of skill and enthusiasm. Similarly, a freelance writer in Vietnam attended a local storytelling night and was approached by a business owner seeking help to revamp their brand's narrative. Unplanned interactions reveal that true opportunity often comes when least expected. Staying approachable, taking on projects with passion, and not dismissing informal chances can lead to significant career moves. Each unexpected offer deserves thoughtful consideration, weighing instinct, adventure, and practicality in balance.

## The Say Yes Philosophy

Adopting a mindset that favors acceptance over hesitation unlocks doors to growth and self-discovery. Opportunities may arrive unannounced: an invitation to a traditional wedding, a suggestion to join a team sport, a last-minute road trip with acquaintances. A British expat found her interest in hiking thanks to a spontaneous invitation to explore mountain trails outside Seoul. Along the way, she discovered a love for nature photography, later exhibiting her work at local events. In another case, saying yes to helping organize a neighborhood celebration led an introverted architect in Italy to form bonds that became the foundation of his social life. By giving a positive response to new experiences—even when they feel awkward or intimidating—people reshape their comfort zone. The resulting confidence and flexibility stay with them, long after the initial leap.

## Reflection and Storytelling

When recognized as more than lucky breaks, serendipitous hap-
penings become powerful ingredients for ongoing personal growth.
Processing the meaning behind these events—whether by journaling, sharing with friends, or simply taking quiet moments of reflection—helps shape perspective. These memories transform into vibrant stories that can inspire others and become a core part of one's
identity. Over time, the ability to spot the value in the unexpected
turns daily life abroad from routine survival into a rich tapestry of
adventure, meaning, and continuous transformation.

## Collecting and Reflecting on Stories: Documenting Your Expat Adventure

Daily journaling transforms fleeting moments and minor surprises
into lasting insight and self-understanding. In the context of expat
life, where every day can bring unexpected discovery, keeping a journal is less about writing lengthy reflections and more about building
consistency. A set ten-minute window each evening—after dinner or
just before bed—creates a gentle rhythm. Some days may call for a
few sentences, others for several paragraphs. The aim is regularity and
honesty rather than perfection or eloquence.

Journaling invites you to see the hidden logic or humor in confusion and mishaps, such as a misunderstanding at a grocery store or the
first time a local idiom stumps a conversation. Prompts offer structure
and fresh perspectives. Rotating questions like "What challenged me
today?" "How did I support or connect with someone in my new
community?" or "What surprised me in my adopted city?" encourage
openness. One day, you might describe the pride in finally navigating

local transit solo; on another, the frustration and laughter of ordering the wrong dish in a new language. Tracking these moments reveals patterns in emotional responses, notes early friendships growing, and charts subtle shifts in confidence or perspective—even the imperceptible transformation that happens through simple days. Reviewing past entries every few weeks to spot recurring themes or evolving attitudes gives depth to your adventure, illuminating the small, repeated steps that underpin larger leaps of growth.

Creative photo projects offer a different kind of record, blending observation and intentional storytelling. Strolling with camera in hand, or just using your phone, you can choose a theme that resonates with your story. "Faces" might mean capturing the bakery worker's daily smile, or the expressions of fellow commuters on a rainy Monday. Selecting "places" keeps your eyes open for unexpected corners: a mural behind the market, a park bench that becomes a favorite thinking spot, a coffee cup left on a windowsill. Other themes might focus on "moments," seeking out spontaneous street performances, drifting autumn leaves along a canal, or the first time you see a familiar street filled with lanterns for a festival. Each photograph deserves a line or two of context written in a notebook or digital app—what the weather smelled like, the tune playing in the background, a mood or private reflection. Compiling these images—filed by week, theme, or emotion—visually maps your journey, revealing how observation sharpens over time. Patterns emerge: how a neighborhood café changes with the seasons, how passing faces become familiar, how the city's pulse is reframed by your own growing comfort. The camera's lens becomes a practice in presence and gratitude, and assembling these photo essays helps you trace your sense of place and belonging.

Voice memos catch emotional texture and fleeting insight that sometimes pass before pen meets paper or thumbs find keyboard.

The voice—undaunted by grammar or spelling—captures laughter, frustration, awe. Each time you experience an unfamiliar taste, fumble through a cultural nuance, or grapple with loneliness or pride, pausing to speak into your phone preserves genuine emotion. Naming the files by mood, date, or event keeps things organized—folders marked "Firsts," "Challenges," or "Little Wins" collect your audio snapshots. Short, spontaneous recordings may hold the tremble of nerves before a job interview, the excitement of a festival's music in the background, or whispered thoughts walking home after an unexpected encounter. Once a month, create a ritual of listening back. This review process reveals how tentative questions in early recordings morph into confidence or understanding. Sometimes, subtle shifts in inflection or perspective illuminate resilience and adaptation that would otherwise fade from memory.

Messages to your future self offer a deliberate way to mark milestones, setbacks, and everything in between. Write a note or record a message on the day you arrive in a new city, after your first difficult negotiation in another language, or when you complete a year abroad. Allocate future dates to revisit these: the next birthday, New Year's Eve, or the second anniversary of your move. These missives serve two key functions. They boost motivation by reminding you of intentions and dreams during moments of fatigue or doubt. They also provide a concrete measure of growth—reading or listening later, you witness how anxiety faded amid new friendships, how homesickness gave way to routine, how a setback became a source of pride. That first job offer or lonely evening transforms, in hindsight, into a marker of how far you've come.

All four practices—journaling, photography, voice recordings, and messages to your future self—build a patchwork of narrative and reflection. As each day's story is collected, interpreted, and revisited, ordinary experience becomes a wellspring for insight, creating a living map of transformation within the adventure of expatriate life.

## Bringing It All Together

Now that we understand how adventure can be found in everyday moments, chance encounters, and unexpected opportunities abroad, we can approach life in a new culture with openness and curiosity. By embracing micro-adventures, taking small social risks, and intentionally documenting our experiences through journaling, photography, or voice memos, we transform ordinary days into meaningful steps of personal growth. This mindset prepares us not only to navigate challenges but also to recognize and welcome the surprises that enrich our journey. Moving forward, cultivating presence and reflection will deepen our connection to place and community, turning the adventure of living abroad into a lasting story of resilience, discovery, and belonging.

# The Triumphant Return: Integrating the Expat Experience

"Coming home felt like stepping into a stranger's story," Lara confessed one evening as she traced the worn edges of a photograph. It wasn't the place that had changed—it was her. The familiar streets, voices, and routines no longer fit the person she had become abroad. Many returning expats face this quiet disruption, where belonging feels uncertain and the past abroad casts long shadows over the present. This tension is not a sign of failure, but a complex marker of growth that few expect. Understanding this experience shifts the narrative from confusion to clarity, revealing how transformation abroad shapes life's unfolding chapters in unexpected ways.

## Navigating Reverse Culture Shock and Applying Lifelong Lessons

Stepping through a front door that once meant comfort, a returning expat may feel like a guest in someone else's life. The neighborhood café greets them with familiar aromas, yet the faces and phrases carry a distance that unsettles the heart. The homecoming's strangeness can appear in small ways: hesitation over which side of the road to walk on, impatience with casual jokes about foreign cultures, or a fleeting sense of loss while browsing local grocery shelves with fewer options than the bustling markets abroad. Once effortless routines now highlight a new sense of separation. This invisible barrier doesn't mean failure to readjust but reflects an internal transformation—a shaped identity that no longer fits into old molds.

Reverse culture shock often starts as a subtle tug of discomfort that grows louder in daily life. A dinner table turns tense when stories from abroad meet polite nods rather than real interest. Friends crack jokes and expect laughter, but the returning expat finds them out of sync, struggling to recognize themselves in the reflection these interactions offer. Emotional fatigue sets in, marked by irritation at small inefficiencies or sadness in the face of past friendships that now feel hollow. Their own city can appear foreign, sparking confusion—shouldn't coming home feel easier than leaving in the first place? These feelings arise not from personal shortcomings, but as signposts of growth and changed perspective.

## Recognizing and Accepting Reentry Symptoms

Identifying reverse culture shock starts with naming the signs. For some, it begins with impatience toward home routines or nostalgic yearning for the customs of distant places. Others notice difficulty in expressing themselves when conversations with loved ones falter. There may be frustration over being misunderstood, or guilt over failing to feel grateful for comforts they once missed. By tuning into these reactions, expats can avoid self-criticism, understanding that grief for lost adventures and anxiety about fitting in are natural phases.

Acceptance becomes crucial. One practical strategy involves journaling daily experiences, which helps to externalize tangled emotions and spot recurring patterns. Setting aside time for personal reflection—perhaps through quiet walks or meditation—gives space for processing. Naming the discomfort transforms it from a personal flaw to a transitional milestone, reducing its emotional weight. By seeking out others who have navigated similar paths, expats discover solidarity and reassurance. Compassion for oneself in this stage is essential, offering patience as identity and expectations settle into a new harmony.

## Everyday Signs of Reverse Culture Shock

- Overreacting to small cultural differences at home

- Reluctance to commit to social events with old friends

- Feeling out of place at family gatherings

- Fantasizing about returning abroad rather than embracing the present

- Difficulty describing unique experiences without feeling boastful or misunderstood

## Sharing Transformation with Friends and Family

Articulating changed perspectives requires conscious effort. A returning expat may find themselves frustrated when new attitudes—such as respect for slower meals or discomfort with constant digital connection—clash with the routines of friends and family. Instead of launching into stories that may seem remote, offering concrete examples helps: "In Japan, I learned to enjoy silence during meals. It made me realize how much I value those moments here, too." This approach grounds personal change in relatable context.

Fostering mutual growth comes from active listening as well as sharing. Inviting questions, opening dialogues, and showing curiosity about loved ones' changes build bridges. A family member may never understand the thrill of a midnight bus ride across a foreign country, but they can appreciate the resilience and humor earned along the way. These conversations, though sometimes awkward, strengthen bonds and nurture empathy on both sides.

## Integrating New Habits and Attitudes

Habits shaped abroad need not be abandoned. A fondness for midday walks might mesh with local parks, while culinary discoveries enrich family meals at home. Practicing learned languages—even if only in private moments or with other speakers online—sustains the joy of communication. Incorporating mindfulness or gratitude rituals, once tied to a European square or a South American café, can transform even ordinary spaces into sanctuaries of calm and self-awareness.

Flexibility proves vital: habits may require adjustment to fit new realities. Seeking out new experiences at home, cultivating curiosity for the local culture, or maintaining an open mindset toward differences help preserve the vitality gained overseas. Each adaptation becomes a thread weaving past journeys into present routines.

## Cultivating a New Sense of Home

'Home' grows beyond place, rooting itself in relationships, self-knowledge, and trust in adaptability. A cup of tea shared with an old friend, small traditions revived at home, or new friendships that begin with stories exchanged—all nurture belonging. Rather than aiming to "fit in," expats can embrace the evolving contours of identity, finding joy in being both grounded and ever-changing.

Adapting to life after international experience builds a toolkit for the future—curiosity, flexibility, stronger relationships, and a comfort with uncertainty offer confidence for whatever comes next.

## Deciding Where Next: Reflective Choices and Global Identity

On a rainy evening in Tokyo, Lara sat at her kitchen table, surrounded by notes with phrases like "family Sunday dinners" and "urban solitude." She was wading through the swirl of whether to return to her birth country, remain in Japan, or search for a new adventure. One practical step she took was a self-assessment worksheet, separating feelings from facts. To use this method yourself, start by writing two columns: one for what supports you where you are—friendships, daily routines, career growth; another for what restricts—distance from family, language challenges, visa worries. Next, list out what "home" means for you right now. Is it familiarity, culture, people, stability? Are there new values or joys you have discovered abroad—a taste for local festivals, a habit of solo travel, a love of languages?

After listing these elements, highlight each with a color: blue for emotional ties, green for practical needs. Lara saw that the longing for "home" pulled her with nostalgia for family, but many daily joys—late-night ramen with friends, cycling safe city streets—held a different weight. She noticed her restlessness for adventure masked fear about being stationary, not just missing her country. Try circling the items on your lists that tug at your heart, then underline the parts you could change or adapt, no matter where you are. This separation of emotion from necessity helps clarify why you're drawn or pushed in a certain direction.

When it came time to choose among real destinations, Nick, a remote-working graphic designer, found his mind spinning with possibilities—accept a job offer in his home city, move to Lisbon with an active expat scene, or stay in Chiang Mai for its affordable lifestyle. To cut through the fog, he used a decision matrix. Start by defining criteria important to your next phase: career advancement, social connection, work-life balance, healthcare quality, cost of living. Write these down as columns. In each row, list a potential destination. Next, score each location from 1 to 5 for every criterion, based on your research or honest gut feeling. For example, Nick rated Lisbon a 5 for social connection, 3 for cost, and 4 for career opportunity. Back home, the job promotion scored high for career (5), lower for social life (2), and moderate for cost (3). Tally totals for each place. Nick realized the pull of the promotion was strong, but Lisbon's vibrant friendships and balance tipped the scale. He could revisit his scoring after speaking with friends or colleagues, making adjustments as new insights emerged.

To bring these decisions to life, practical steps smooth the path. Begin by drafting a checklist split by category: paperwork (visas, residency, taxes), finances (bank accounts, savings allocations, insurance), housing (temporary stays, long-term leases), timelines (key dates for moving, deadlines for applications), and social support (professional contacts, expat groups, schools or childcare). Tick off each item as you gather information or make arrangements. Early on, Ana and her partner decided to move their family from Berlin to Melbourne. They mapped out their children's school registration deadlines, surveyed neighborhoods for family-friendly parks, and identified local international communities through social media and school newsletters. By setting mini deadlines—booking flights, shipping possessions, organizing video tours of prospective homes—they reduced last-minute pressure and enabled their children to preview the upcoming change through photos and online introductions with local kids. These steps created a bridge from old routines to new beginnings.

Once the lists and logistics are underway, take a step back to acknowledge how the patterns of moving and adapting have transformed your sense of self. Visualize each place you've called home as adding a thread to your personal tapestry. Invite yourself to describe, in a journal entry or mind map, what you have gained from each cultural setting—new worldviews, language snippets, ways of greeting strangers, tastes for unfamiliar foods. For example, Maya's mind map connected British humor from London, Turkish hospitality from Istanbul, and a practical independence honed during her years in Singapore. She wrote a single sentence beside each: "London taught me wit softens awkwardness," "Istanbul taught me patience over tea," "In Singapore, I learned to thrive alone in a crowd." Sketching these connections on paper surfaced pride in the layers she had woven.

Return to your map or sentences. Notice what unique blend has emerged—perhaps a capacity to adapt, an ease with ambiguity, or a delight in connecting stories across continents. Carry this recognition forward, letting curiosity about what you will add next guide you. With each move, each moment of return or renewal, there is wisdom worth sharing and celebrating, pointing toward the ongoing discoveries of your expat adventure.

## Owning and Celebrating Your Expat Story

Moments of growth while living abroad often reveal themselves in unexpected ways. Sometimes, it's the first time you navigate a foreign subway system alone without panic, or when you negotiate a lease in a new language and realize afterward that you not only survived but thrived during the challenge. Recognizing these victories, no matter their scale, grants a powerful sense of accomplishment. Even small acts, like daring to try a new local dish, striking up a conversation with a stranger, or coping with a holiday away from family, contribute to an intricate tapestry of resilience. By naming and owning these achievements—whether bravely speaking up when lost in translation, or enduring waves of homesickness and finding new sources of comfort—expats stitch together proof of their adaptability and resourcefulness.

It helps to make a practice of reflecting on these events. One technique is to jot down specific challenges faced and how you responded, keeping a simple journal or notes on a phone, so that victories can be seen and celebrated. Over time, the cumulative effect of these stories builds self-confidence. Looking back at non-linear progress, you'll notice that each resolved difficulty, from navigating bureaucratic offices to making new friends through meet-ups, becomes proof of grit and courage. These personal milestones become the foundation of motivation for the future, reminding you that the skills learned abroad remain with you for new chapters ahead.

Sharing the journey transforms individual triumph into collective insight. When expats tell their stories—describing the ups and downs, breakthroughs and low points—they help others facing similar situations feel less alone. A French teacher who once struggled through her first months in Seoul uses her tale of confusion over cultural norms and eventual mastery of public etiquette as a bridge to guide new arrivals. By recounting the moment she learned to bow at just the right angle or the time she stumbled over polite phrases in a shop, she offers more than just information; she shares emotional truth. These kinds of stories provide meaning, for both teller and listener, weaving together clarity, humor, and hope.

Mentoring others doesn't always require formal programs. It can be as simple as answering questions on expat forums, listening to a newcomer's nerves during a coffee meet-up, or writing blog posts about the realistic highs and lows of life abroad. Illustrating these examples offers tangible ways to connect: a long-term expat in Germany starts a casual WhatsApp group for fellow international parents to swap survival tips, while another leads walking tours in their adopted city, revealing practical knowledge and insider views. Each act helps newcomers develop empathy and confidence as they navigate their own transitions.

Giving back to the expatriate community amplifies the sense of belonging and accomplishment for everyone involved. Encouraging a colleague who's just arrived from overseas, sharing links to useful resources, or creating a simple checklist for registering with local authorities may seem small, but can be a lifeline to someone feeling overwhelmed. Some expats choose to volunteer as cultural liaisons at schools or businesses, recognizing that helping others adapt not only eases their journey but deepens their own roots in the new community. Offering mentorship—whether formally through organizations or informally through friendships—sustains a supportive network where wisdom is passed along, mistakes are de-stigmatized, and victories are jointly celebrated.

## Ways to Give Back

- Host informal meet-ups for recent arrivals

- Share written guides or tip sheets for everyday challenges

- Create discussion groups about emotional adaptation and culture shock

- Offer to accompany newcomers on important local errands

- Encourage pay-it-forward mentality within networks

Moving out of reflection and into future-driven living demands a commitment to using hard-earned insights as a compass for growth. The confidence built from overcoming adversity abroad inspires a mindset of curiosity and openness in all pursuits. Approaching each new challenge—whether personal or professional—with the same courage and resourcefulness used in unfamiliar countries means that growth becomes a continuous process, not just a chapter left behind.

Practical strategies keep this spirit alive. Setting new cross-cultural learning goals, staying in touch with international friends, reading global news, or simply continuing to engage with unfamiliar perspectives ensures that the values cultivated abroad remain central. The ability to observe without judging too quickly, ask for help without shame, and adapt plans on short notice aren't just skills for the next move; they're principles for lifelong fulfillment and achievement. Claiming each success, supporting others, and living forward with curiosity ties the expat journey into an unending source of inspiration and strength.

## Bringing It All Together

Now that we understand the complex emotions and growth that come with returning home, we can better embrace the ongoing journey of adapting and redefining what "home" means. Recognizing reverse culture shock as a natural part of transformation allows us to approach reentry with patience and self-compassion. By reflecting on lessons learned abroad, sharing our stories, and using practical tools to guide future decisions, we build resilience and confidence for whatever comes next. Owning our unique expat experiences not only honors past challenges but also fuels ongoing personal development, helping us navigate new chapters with openness, curiosity, and a sense of belonging wherever life takes us.

# Epilogue

Years later, Erin stood on a balcony overlooking a city she once feared she would never understand. The streets below no longer felt foreign; the rhythms had become familiar, comforting even. She had stumbled through languages, customs, mistakes, and heartbreak. She had rebuilt routines, friendships, courage, and a sense of self she didn't know she had lost.

She was no longer the woman who boarded that plane—scared, uncertain, and unsure of her place in the world.

She had learned that belonging does not arrive all at once.
It grows in small victories.
It blooms in unexpected friendships.
It awakens in moments of clarity born from struggle.

Home was no longer a single destination.
Home was everywhere she had grown.

And as she looked out at the city lights, she realized something quietly extraordinary:

She had not just survived abroad.
She had *become* abroad.

# Final Thoughts

Life abroad is never a straight path. It is a shifting, unpredictable journey filled with surprises, disappointments, breakthroughs, and moments that reshape your heart. But every challenge you face is proof of your resilience. Every mistake is a step forward. Every unfamiliar moment is a chance to build a new part of yourself.

If there is one truth every expat learns, it is this:

**You do not lose yourself abroad—you meet yourself.**

Carry these stories, insights, and lessons with you as you continue building a life far from home... yet deeply rooted in courage, strength, and hope.

Your journey is only beginning.

# Review Request

**Thank You for Reading!**

Your support means the world. If you enjoyed this book, would you
leave a quick review? Even one sentence helps other readers discover
the story.

★★★ *CLICK HERE TO LEAVE YOUR REVIEW* ★★★

www.ingramcontent.com/pod-product-compliance
Lightning Source LLC
Chambersburg PA
CBHW021116130626
46554CB00002B/714